In the Best Interest of the Patient

Ethical and Legal Issues in the Practice of Psychotherapy

Barbara Lipinski, Ph.D.

First printing, April, 1999

Published by
Pacific Meridian Center
301 Los Cabos Lane
Ventura, CA 93001

Copies may be ordered directly from
Pacific Meridian Center
(805) 641-1368

Library of Congress Card Catalog Number 99-90292
In the best interest of the patient: Ethical and legal issues in the practice of psychotherapy / Barbara Lipinski.
Includes bibliographic references and index.

1. Psychotherapists-Professional ethics. 2. Psychotherapy-Ethics. 3. Counselors-Professional ethics.
I. Lipinski, Barbara. II. Title.

ISBN Number 1-928702-02-3

Printed in the United States of America by

1117 First Avenue SE, Cedar Rapids, IA 52404, 1-800-301-4545

To the memory of Alicja and Janek,
my mother and father

And to all who engage in the struggle for integrity

Reprint Permissions

CONTENTS

Part One: Introduction

Part Two: Ethical and Legal Issues

Part Three: Vignette Conceptualization

PREFACE

Ethics and the practice of psychotherapy are undeniably woven together within this text. Imagine for a moment, a willow tree obtaining its nourishment from the forest floor, a well composted soil hosting different organisms, its roots reaching deeply into the earth, and its trunk, branches, and leaves exchanging the necessary nutrients with the air surrounding it. The tree exists within an entire ecosystem where energy flows in and out.

Akin to the willow tree, the fluent practice of psychotherapy actively grows out of an ethical sphere, which itself grows and changes. The ethical structure is composed of professional codes of ethics, standards of practice, laws, and one's own character and moral development. Add to this a therapist's formative years of education, training, and experience within the field of psychotherapy, and the result is an organic ethos. A living professional field of aspirations and prohibitions, a diverse community engaged in active discussion and at times, agreement on practice and appropriate behavior.

With this intention, the work on the following pages reflects an organic perspective, subject to ongoing consideration, revision, and further integration. Practicing with integrity is challenging and calls upon complex decision making processes centered around the best interest of the patient. As Guggenbuhl-Craig stated "It is our sacred duty to investigate continually how a patient can be helped and how harm can be avoided" (1995, p. viii). These challenges and investigations are given a voice here.

Intended Audience

This text is written for individuals practicing psychotherapy, studying psychotherapy, teaching psychotherapy from the perspective of actively integrating ethics and legal standards, and preparing for oral presentations and licensing examinations. Psychotherapists are primarily trained in clinical or counseling psychology, marriage and family therapy, psychiatry, and clinical social work. They may be skilled in brief solution focused counseling methods, problem solving models, narrative approaches, and long term depth oriented psychotherapy or analysis. Regardless of the specific approach, discipline, theoretical orientation, or training, each therapist is required to function in an ethically appropriate and facilitative manner in their work with patients or clients.

Resources

Resources are included to assist professionals who seek more information on child abuse, domestic violence, sexual assault, trauma, child custody, elder abuse, and dependent adult abuse. Ancillary information on professional associations and national clearinghouses for clinical and research information are listed as well as 24 hour hotlines or information lines for patient use.

For those intrigued by continuing the integration of law and mental health information on child custody evaluations and the practice of mediation is offered. Crucial differences exist between therapeutic and forensic relationships, such as the rules governing privilege (Greenberg & Shuman, 1997), thus psychotherapists wishing to expand their practice should obtain rigorous training in these new areas of practice. Independent practitioners may utilize their professional skills in these forensic areas, which require a solid foundation in listening skills, an understanding of developmental issues and family dynamics, the ability to engage in critical analyses and assessments of complex situations, and a proficient grasp of ethical and legal standards. Both of these specialties welcome skilled psychotherapists. Last, the Ethical Principles for Psychologists and Code of Conduct and the Ethical Standards for Marriage and Family Therapists are located in the Appendix for reference purposes.

Terminology

Throughout this work, I have favored the term patient rather than client, although the terms may be used interchangeably by the reader. In exploring the historical derivations of each word (Oxford Dictionary of English Etymology, 1966), I believe patient "enduring or suffering" (p. 657), is in agreement with my view of the transformative process of psychotherapy. C. G. Jung (1954) described an endeavor of psychotherapy as assisting the patient to learn how to authentically bear suffering and to "acquire steadfastness and philosophic patience in face of suffering" (p. 81). The term client denotes a function of the role, such as a customer, or "one for whom professional services are rendered" (Webster's II New Riverside University Dictionary, 1984, p. 270). Feel free to use the term that expresses your perspective best.

Format

Part One addresses the foundational principle of practicing in the best interest of the patient, introduces the realm of ethical practice, presents decision making models, offers information on protean standards of care, and encourages a tolerance for ambiguity. Part Two highlights the more prominent ethical and legal issues integral to the practice of psychotherapy. An emphasis on California law is provided. Part Three offers methods for conceptualizing vignettes and cases to be used within practice, for case presentations, and in oral examination situations. A section on therapist self-care is offered to address longevity in this profession.

Acknowledgments

Inspiration comes in many forms, cloaked in both challenge and awe. For this work, inspiration arrived in the form of many inquisitive students. I offer thanks to all the gifted graduate students who have rigorously queried me about their ethical responsibilities, legal duties, and decision making processes in psychotherapy. I remain grateful to Pacifica Graduate Institute for providing me the opportunity to teach this material for the past nine years.

A supportive community has sustained me, allowing for the creation of this text. I am most thankful for the expert guidance of Richard Leslie, JD, attorney for the California Association of Marriage and Family Therapists, and Mary Riemersma, MBA, Executive Director, who have willingly answered a myriad of legal questions since the early 1980's.

In deep appreciation, I give special thanks to Eithne Jackman for her immense support and open generosity and Nina Falls for her remarkable sense of humor and heartfelt encouragement. I also note the graceful impact of these special teachers: Dr. Frank Fox, Thich Nhat Hanh, and Pema Chodron.

I am appreciative of working relationships with several people, who have modeled a style of ethical decision making that serves as a framework for my personal style: Bob Sauter, LCSW, former Mental Health Evaluation Manager at Santa Barbara County Mental Health Administration; the Honorable Yale Coggan, JD, retired judge and former Santa Barbara County hearing officer for habeus corpus certification review hearings; and Dr. Mary Watkins, depth psychologist, who has deeply affected me through her gentle, compassionate, and soulful manner in addressing issues of conflict.

I am also thankful for the support of many professional colleagues, including Dr. Phil Snyder, Peggy Zorn, MA, Dr. Lionel Corbett, Dr. Dennis Slattery, Dr. Cathy Rives, Dr. Helene Lorenz, Dr. Charles Asher, Dr. Dianne Skafte, and Dr. Steve Aizenstat. I owe a debt of gratitude to Dr. Jacqueline Bouhoutsos, creator of Post-Therapy Groups for individuals who were sexually involved with therapists; and the host of

Minnesota professionals who pioneered the legislation regarding therapist sexual relationships.

In retrospect, I am grateful to all those I have had the opportunity to know through the story of their struggles with ethical decision making. These most difficult and trying situations have contributed to my current perspective on ethics, decision making, and professional practice in psychotherapy. I sincerely thank you.

PART ONE: INTRODUCTION

In the Best Interest of the Patient

A fundamental principle of ethical practice in psychotherapy is honored within this text, best summed up with the phrase in *the best interest of the patient*. How easily we lose sight of the best interest of the patient when struggling with the myriad of ethical and legal obligations that arise within psychotherapy or when relying solely on good intentions or the principles of self-protection and risk management. Consider this scenario during an initial session:

> Elena tearfully describes her sorrow over the ending of her marriage, and relates her confusion around her husband's betrayal. She mentions how vulnerable and powerless she feels, as she did in her childhood. She's not even sure she can trust you. She reveals her ambivalence about taking any action in the ensuing divorce, but knows she must do something. She provides information about her husband, a psychotherapist, indicating he is involved sexually with a current patient. As she struggles to speak, you realize you met her husband at an ethics committee meeting last week. Near the end of the session, Elena wonders how she ever fell in love with her husband, who was her therapist just two years ago. You learn their sexual relationship began during therapy, and Elena originally sought treatment for issues related to incest. She prefers that you bill her husband for the psychotherapy.

The complexities slowly become apparent: issues of boundary violations, attachment, betrayal, confidentiality, and distrust emerge. Questions about competence to treat, informed consent and billing arrangements, scope of practice, potentials of danger to self or others, potential cross-cultural issues, and conflicts of interest arise. You are fully aware of ethical responsibilities to your patient, the foremost being confidentiality, and you are aware that no breach of confidentiality is permitted in this instance. You have a responsibility to provide the patient with the brochure *Professional therapy never includes sex* (California Department of Consumer Affairs, 1997) and you are required to discuss the contents. You'll need to conduct a thorough assessment and potentially consider issues of danger to self and others. You also plan to explore the extent of the potential conflict of interest in serving on an ethics committee with her husband.

One of the first considerations at hand is whether this is a case you may take or may need to refer to a more competent practitioner who does not have any conflicts of interest. If you can ethically take the case, what is your responsibility to inform your patient of your ethics committee involvement, especially in light of her situation and history? Do you decide to terminate your ethics committee involvement? Can you ethically bill her husband for the treatment? What is your fee payment policy regarding who is responsible for the bill? How will these decisions impact the therapeutic process? What actions are in the best interest of the patient?

As you begin to discern your responsibilities in this case, you review the central focus on acting in the best interest of the patient, which includes respecting autonomy, beneficence, nonmaleficence or doing no harm, and fairness, combined with accepting accountability for your actions. Through this lens of integrity, you begin to view your actions, responsibilities, and potential consequences in a new light. With integrity as a partner, you proceed consciously and openly as you reflect on the alternatives in this situation. Perhaps revisiting your material on ethics, engaging in further research, and consulting with a colleague will assist you in the decision making process.

In affirming the importance of integrity, Grudin (1990) defined this construct as "psychological and ethical wholeness" (p. 75) continuing over time, integrating the reality of an external situation with an expression of one's internal thoughts and desires. I find this complementary nature of the inner and outer realities crucial to the process of ethically appropriate behavior and decision making. For example, a formal ethical code of behavior can be construed as an external reality, engaged with on an internal level by the practitioner of psychotherapy. This is a complex process requiring the therapist to be actively and experientially involved in an exploration, through what Jung (1971) proposed as the functions of consciousness: thinking, intuition, sensation, and feeling. This dialectic of integrity differs from a blind acceptance and adherence to a set of codified rules.

Occasionally, making decisions in the best interest or interests of your patient may include engaging in legally and ethically permitted or mandated breaches of confidentiality. At other times engaging in a legal mandate, such as a court order to reveal information at the risk of being charged with contempt of court, may be in opposition to an ethical standard, requiring a more complex process to discern the answer to the question, "Is this in the best interest of my patient?"

Therapists who are solely guided by their good intentions commit egregious errors by transgressing boundaries and violating ethical principles, standards, and laws. Through my service on ethics committees, I have encountered individuals who articulate their own unique ethos, often believed to be a superior morality, eschewing the generally accepted group ethic or clear legal standard. For example, initiating a sexual relationship with a patient, or believing that physical touch and massage is a necessary calming component in a first session with an incest survivor, regardless of the literature contrary to the subject (Briere, 1989; Hunter & Struve, 1998; Pope & Bouhoutsos, 1986). Conversely, to be guided solely by the defensive posture of the risk management perspective, resulting in the attribution of negative intentions to patient behavior (believed to be driven by a litigious society), contributes to a fearful and protective stance within psychotherapy, limiting therapeutic effectiveness. An approach to ethics integrating an introspective approach with the continuous development of one's intellectual and emotional competence, added to an acknowledgment and assessment of the best interests of the patient provides a more balanced perspective.

Many are familiar with the Hippocratic oath initiated around 400 BCE. Considered the father of medical ethics, Hippocrates offered two precepts which are foundational in psychotherapeutic practice today: confidentiality and the obligation to do no harm to patients. The standard of maintaining confidentiality and the attitude of nonmaleficence (do no harm) are well integrated into ethical codes of conduct in the healing arts professions. These provide a solid grounding for working in the best interest of the patient. This text integrates these and other standards and aspirations found in the codes of professional associations, including the American Psychological Association and the California Association of Marriage and Family Therapists.

The Realm of Ethical Practice

A profound pleasure is waiting to be experienced in the realm of ethical practice. I believe there are opportunities for immense personal growth when challenged with an ethical dilemma. For some therapists these experiences may be acutely painful, for others intriguing and perhaps thought provoking. At best the outcome is favorable to all parties concerned, at its worst, the outcome can be harmful to a patient's life and the therapist's livelihood. My aim is to present the benefits of mindfully attending to ethical issues while keeping the patient's best interest at heart.

The Myers-Briggs Type Indicator (Myers & Briggs, 1976) is an assessment instrument widely used in organizational psychology to measure individual personality dispositions and preferences. The dispositions are assessed on continuums of extroversion-introversion (relating more to the external or internal world), sensation-intuition (how one takes information in), thinking-feeling (how one prefers to make choices and decisions), and judging-perceiving (utilizing a more evaluative or receptive framework). An individual is characterized as having one of the 16 personality types.

I emerge as an individual with the following type: INFP, or introverted, intuitive, feeling, and perceiving. These personality preferences, or ways of being in the world, are quite revealing, indicating strengths and weaknesses. For example, it is true that I enjoy being challenged, welcoming experiences that broaden my perceptions, allowing for more possibilities in life. I may initially reflect on an issue through an inner exploration noting the nature and meaning of the experience or I may engage in a journal writing process, noting my emotional and intuitive response. In terms of decision making, the possibilities can be endless when I think through a dilemma. For this reason, I challenge myself with others' opinions, logically and systematically thinking through the details of the situation and discussing these, and evaluating the varying courses of action. Ultimately, the outcome of my action will be a combination of the exploratory processes I engaged in, but will likely reflect my personality style.

Awareness of my personality style assists me in acknowledging that I may prefer to work out issues in a particular manner, with personal reflection and a reliance on feelings and intuitive processes. This style could be seen as a personal limitation, thus in an ethical dilemma or conflictual situation, it would be prudent to challenge myself by consulting with others, and discussing their opinions in logical and systematic ways. This provides a system of checks and balances in the decision making process.

In addition to stylistic preferences, the process of making sound ethical decisions involves a number of steps, beginning with education. The training in ethics received in graduate school will serve as a foundational base. But the educational process cannot end there. Ethical codes are updated and new laws are frequently introduced, requiring careful review and integration. Learning methods for analyzing complex ethical dilemmas may also be helpful. Unique or novel issues that are rarely encountered may require a new strategy for decision making, more information, or expert consultation. Education is usually the initial step, but it should also serve as an ongoing process in your career. Continuing educational efforts will keep you well informed of the guidelines for ethical and competent professional conduct.

Becoming aware of an ethical problem

There are a number of excellent decision making models to employ when encountering an ethical dilemma. But how do you know there is an ethical dilemma? What is the process of making something that is relatively unknown, known? Even with the foundational education on ethics, we can encounter our personal blind spots, or have hidden biases, limitations, lack of knowledge, insight, or awareness about an issue. Professionals also differ substantially in the way they become aware of ethical dilemmas. As Gilligan's studies (1982) of moral development indicated, the very conception of ethical conduct, such as identification of rights and responsibilities, evolves from maturational experiences which are related to gender role. Although she postulated two disparate modes of experience she described a reality common to both men and women "the fact that in life you never see it all, that things unseen undergo change through time, that there is more than one path to gratification, and that the boundaries between self and other are less clear than they sometimes seem" (Gilligan, 1982, p. 172). Her studies significantly broadened the literature on moral development (Kohlberg, 1981) and the sequencing of moral decision making in the resolution of conflict in human relationships.

Given that we are likely unaware of some dilemmas, I recommend joining a professional association (see Appendix), becoming familiar with the monthly literature, reading journals, attending conferences or workshops, and seeking consultation and/or personal psychotherapy when faced with the inevitable anxiety that accompanies a transgression of integrity. Fortunately the unsettling experience of an ethical breach resulting in feelings of anxiety, may lead to the rediscovery of one's integrity (Beebe, 1995). At a minimum this practice enhances our perspective on professional issues, and may assist us in becoming aware of an issue we might not otherwise be aware of. Of course, once aware of these unsettling anxious feelings, we can employ a heuristic research model (Moustakas, 1990) to investigate and discover the source. This involves self-search, self-dialogue, and self-discovery. Regularly attending continuing education seminars on the subtleties of ethical dilemmas and decision making would be another helpful intervention.

Becoming aware of ethical issues can lead to framing the right question (Canter, Bennett, Jones, & Nagy, 1994). Asking the right question can assist in a meaningful exploration of any potential conflict of interest, assessments about level of competence, and scope of training, education, or experience. For example, "Do I have the necessary education and experience to treat this particular disorder?" or "Will providing psychotherapy to this patient present a conflict of interest in any way," or "Am I altering my customary ways of practice with this patient?" Clearly framing the right question is a developmental skill that is built on throughout one's professional career.

This brings to mind the internal supervision model proposed by Casement (1991). Briefly, as we gain more experience, work with varying supervisors, and consult with different professionals, we develop inner personal supervisory models that assist us in assessing and monitoring our professional behavior. From a self-psychological perspective a revealing parallel concept to this experience is the process of transmuting internalization (Kohut, 1984), or simply stated, integrating one's therapist, or in this case one's supervisor, as a self-object. Thus an active and effective internal supervisor is vital to our work, continually enhanced or modified based on successive experiences, and may allow for the articulation of the right questions.

There are various methods available to employ in the complex decision making process involved in potential ethical dilemmas. This next section presents several decision making models.

Ethical Decision Making

Personality style will influence the methods we use and the choices we make when faced with ethical issues. Let's assume that you have become aware of an ethical dilemma, and you wish to resolve it appropriately and in the best interest of your patient. As an example, imagine the following:

> After the third session of psychotherapy with Maury, a struggling young man who recently sought political asylum in the United States, you pick up messages from the answering service. An individual identifying himself as a close friend of your patient's wishes to pay for the psychotherapy and serve as a benefactor, but without Maury's knowledge. He mentions that he has already mailed a sizable check to serve as a retainer.

You are essentially an ethical person and desire to apply your personal standards of integrity in this situation. You are not motivated by the potential punishment or penalty for not acting appropriately, but aspire to a higher level of ethical behavior. Let's examine the potential problem first. An unknown third party has sent an advance payment for Maury's psychotherapy, and wishes that this fact remain hidden from Maury. We know that even the fact of a psychotherapeutic relationship is to be held in confidence. We also know that Maury is paying a minimal fee that was negotiated at the beginning of therapy. Perhaps we are uncovering a potential conflict here.

Let's apply Kitchener's (1984) critical-evaluative model to help find a direction for our ethical decision making. In this model, four moral principles are reviewed: 1) autonomy, 2) beneficence, 3) nonmaleficence, and 4) justice and fairness. We begin with autonomy, which indicates a patient has a right and the freedom to make his or her own informed decisions. Second, beneficence refers to the contribution towards growth and the general welfare of the patient and the active prevention of harm. Another way to imagine this is to think of promoting the welfare of a patient. Third, nonmaleficence refers to the maxim "do no harm" which calls on therapists to avoid harming patients and not engaging in risks to do so. And fourth, justice and fairness refers to the provision of equitable treatment for all patients.

With Maury's situation, it seems clear that we would not promote self-determination if we made a decision on behalf of Maury and simply accepted the money, or did not share this information with him. In order to do so, Maury would need to be told of this phone call and make an informed decision. Second, how would we be promoting good on behalf of the patient, if we accepted the check or did not disclose this to him? We are now beginning to see that such an act lacks integrity and might prove harmful. Third, how is our possible action a potential risk for Maury? At what cost to the therapeutic relationship? Is this benefactor a friend? And fourth, we review this principle of justice and fairness, to see if we are affording equal treatment to Maury, as we would with any other patient.

Add a fifth principle: Best interest - is this action in the best interest of my patient? What decisions would be in his best interest? It is not in Maury's best interest to disrespect his autonomy, or to engage in dishonest behavior which has a potential for harm. Since the therapeutic contract is between Maury and yourself, you have decided to resolve this potential conflict by discussing the phone call with him and returning the check. As Gottlieb (1994) has indicated ethical decision making and solid professional judgment reciprocally influence each other.

Another systematic ethical decision making model was proposed by Keith-Spiegel and Koocher (1985). This model involves sequential steps encompassing a description of the parameters of the situation, a definition of issues, consultation with guidelines, an evaluation of rights and responsibilities of the involved parties, brainstorming alternate decisions, citing the consequences of each decision, presenting evidence that consequences or benefits will occur, then making the decision. Developing alternatives and examining them carefully for both the potential benefits and consequences can provide quite a comprehensive picture of the impact on the patient and any other significant figures in the dilemma. Tymchuk (1986) developed a similar problem solving model, with a focus on the short-term and long-term consequences of the decision, and the psychological, social, and economic costs associated with the implementation of each alternative. This is referred to as a cost-benefit analysis.

Let us move on to a more complex situation, which we explore with another method. The following scenario unfolds at your new employment site:

> You are seeing patients during your first week at an outpatient clinic in the city you have just moved to. On Friday, a patient referred by his employment assistance program (which has a contract with your clinic) anxiously

describes a situation where he witnessed his next door neighbor's child being sexually abused two months ago in his condominium playlot, and acknowledged he was a mandated reporter, but had not made the report. You recognize the mandate to make a child sexual abuse report, but as a probationary employee, decide to review the procedure with your supervisor first. Your supervisor has left for the day, so you consult with the associate director, also a licensed therapist, who instructs you not to make a report since the patient is a well known city councilman and the publicity could hurt the clinic.

The feminist model for ethical decision making combines the traditional rational and evaluative models described earlier, with three other factors: recognition of the power differential that exists between the therapist and patient; the therapist's intuitive and emotional response; and the awareness of any cultural biases embedded within the decision making process (Hill, Glaser, & Harden, 1995). This model integrates the social context of the issue.

With the above case, if one examines the issues from the rational evaluative and an intuitive emotional stance, a number of issues arise: clear mandate to report with reasonable suspicion, patient's trust and perhaps expectations of reporting in sharing this information with you (this can be explored directly with the patient); the administrative workplace aspect regarding the director's prohibition. Your intuitive and emotional response may provide valuable information about the situation you are in, including the political climate and ethics of the agency. And the best interest of the patient includes the clinical dynamics of this case: the patient has come forward, perhaps with a range of feelings about not reporting and is now seeking assistance in this matter. Exploring these issues, the options available to the patient, and your reporting responsibilities can result in an empowering decision for the patient.

An Integrative Model

I'd like to present the facts of a brief ethical dilemma followed by an integrative decision making model. The case (adapted from Pope & Vasquez, 1998) is presented here for you to struggle with the issues, reflect on your responses, and to hopefully challenge your decision making process. Please imagine yourself as the treating clinician, including the empathic and caring relationship that has developed between you and the patient, then apply some of the steps of the integrative model to this dilemma.

> During the fourth month of psychotherapy with an eighteen year old patient, you learn he has been diagnosed with an inoperable spinal tumor. In the next six months, he experiences numerous debilitating complications, two hospitalizations, and discovers he has Acquired Immunodeficiency Syndrome, AIDS. In a session he expresses an interest in becoming psychologically and spiritually prepared for his now imminent death. In the next few sessions, he vividly describes where he would like to die and how he will obtain drugs to facilitate his death during those last days. He indicates he will discontinue therapy if you try to dissuade him from his plan.

The following integrative model is proposed for evaluating a dilemma and potential solutions in the patient's best interest. The acronym *REFLECT* assists in remembering these steps: rational aspects, exploration, feelings and intuitive responses, legal issues, ethical guidance, context of the dilemma, and treatment impact. The model is not necessary a linear one, and allows for a re-cycling through several steps.

REFLECT

- Rational
- Exploration
- Feelings
- Legal Issue
- Ethical Code
- Context
- Treatment

Rational Aspects

One begins the process noting the rational aspects of the potential dilemma, viewing the current facts of the matter in a logical and systematic fashion. Some suggested questions to ponder are offered:

- What are the facts in front of me?
- How can I define or articulate the dilemma?
- What is the patient's perception of the problem?
- What is the impact on the patient?
- What do I know about this case and what information is missing ?
- What else do I need to know in order to make an informed decision?
- What is the conflict I see or experience at this point?
- Who is involved in this conflict?

Exploration of Issues & Feelings and Intuitive Responses

The exploration phase moves on to an in depth exploration of the facts of the case. Any feelings or intuitive responses to the issues are noted.

- What is my intuitive response to this dilemma?
- How do my responses and actions inform me?
- What feelings am I aware of?

- Do I have any hesitancies or reservations?
- What are my thoughts, feelings, and images about asking for help?

Legal Standards & Ethical Guidelines

Next, the legal standards are reviewed as well as the ethical guidance provided from one's professional association's ethical codes.

- Is this an ethical or legal dilemma?
- Consult the legal standard for the legal issue.
- Consult the ethics code, identify the ethical principle or standard.
- Consult an attorney, colleague, supervisor, therapist.
- What is the standard of practice for this particular issue in my context of practice?
- What are my duties and responsibilities as I now understand them?
- What are my reflections and responses to this dilemma at this point?

A helpful way to do so, is to look at the particular facts once again, from the legal and ethical perspective. Whether the law or ethical code is clear or ambiguous in terms of the particular issues, we step back and evaluate our overall responses once again, adding another layer of exploration and feeling/intuitions. At this juncture the decision making process may become more fruitful or more chaotic. Seeking consultation at this stage in the decision making process would provide clarity or a differing perspective of the dilemma. The efficacy of consultation from a colleague, supervisor, therapist, and/or an attorney is immeasurable.

Context of Issue & Impact on Treatment

The context of the issue is also explored reviewing the precipitating factors of the dilemma, all the individuals affected by the dilemma and of course, the impact of this dilemma on the treatment process and the patient. An exploration of contextual variables are essential, including the similarities and differences between the patient's and therapist's values or characteristics, such as political views, sexual orientation, gender, class, culture, or religion.

- What is the context of this dilemma?
- Who is affected by this issue (including the patient's family, significant others, or friends)?
- What is the impact on the treatment process?
- If a breach of confidentiality must occur, how best to handle it?
- What is the impact on the patient of this dilemma or developing solution?
- Can I directly collaborate with the patient on this issue and the potential options?
- What is the patient's expressed wish?
- What contextual variables are present? Political views, sexual orientation, gender, class, culture, race, religion, developmental issues.
- What characteristics or biases do I bring to this issue?
- What is in the best interest of the patient?

Solutions

This systematic process continues as possible solutions are generated. The same type of reflective process is employed for the solution to the dilemma with the addition of a criterion analysis. One weighs the options and examines the decisions in reference to the following criterion measure:

Is the solution:
Generalizable
Proclamable,
Equitable?

- Is my solution to this ethical or legal dilemma?

  Generalizable,
  Proclamable, and
  Equitable

Generalizable:

- Would other psychotherapists in my position engage in the same behavior?
- Would this decision be reached by other reasonable psychotherapists?

Proclamable:

- Is this resulting decision something I could confidently and openly share with my colleagues, knowing it was appropriate?
- Will it stand up to public scrutiny among my peers, professional community, and in the legal arena?

Equitable:

- Is this decision just and fair and would it be applied to anyone else regardless of his or her gender, religion, age, culture, ethnicity, race, language, sexual orientation, or economic class?

If the course of action does not result in an affirmative answer to each one of these questions, then an alternative course of action should be chosen. An ongoing reassessment of the dilemma and the effectiveness of the chosen response continues until the psychotherapist has arrived at the best possible solution for all parties.

Implementing a thought provoking exploration such as this, will aid the therapist in arriving at the best possible solution to the ethical or legal dilemma. A significant framework of this decision making process involves a willingness to accept responsibility and the potential consequences of one's decision. Many ethical dilemmas are best reviewed and revisited as situations change, "frequently ethical decisions have an evolving, unfolding quality" (Hill, Glaser, & Harden, 1995, p. 35). These continued opportunities will allow for further exploration resulting in more effective professional practice and refinements in the complex process of decision making.

Protean Standards of Care

Standards of care are duties imposed on psychotherapists. The acceptable standard of care is actually a minimum standard, not a "best" standard, or standard of perfection. A standard of care is formulated on a number dimensions, not one sufficiently comprehensive to solely guide professional responsibility:

1) Statutes, applicable state laws, and federal regulations, such as elder abuse reporting laws;
2) Regulations of the specific licensing boards, such as advertising subtleties, supervision expectations, or training;
3) Court cases, such as Tarasoff;
4) Professional Association's Ethical Codes and Principles;
5) Rules and regulations of the institution where one is employed (e.g., working within the armed forces would require knowledge of the different rules around confidentiality); and
6) Consensus of the professional community.

The consensus of one's professional community is indispensable when contemplating an action that may be questionable. Framing a question such as "Is this act something I would willingly and openly share with my colleagues" or "How would my colleagues react to my decision to follow through with this course of action" or "Is this behavior endorsed within my community" could provide the necessary initial information for your decision making process, particularly if you believe your colleagues would disapprove or oppose your action. Naturally, the next step is to consult with other colleagues within your community, particularly those you believe would disagree with your course of action. Even in terms of ethics cases adjudicated in court, when there is no case law precedent, the standard of care applied to these legal matters is based on the behavior of what similar professionals would do in these instances (Hopkins & Anderson, 1985).

Based on this, the standard of care is at best protean, assuming different forms based on changes in the law, regulations, ethics, and common practice. Perhaps a helpful way to remember this is to think of Proteus, an ancient sea god in Greek mythology, who had the power to change shapes. He spoke oracularly, and would foretell the future, but only if physically held. At will, he would change himself into a lion, a dragon, a panther, into water, fire, a tree, and so on. It was essential not to be intimidated by his metamorphoses, for then, and only then, would Proteus speak. It was considered a propitious moment when he revealed his vision.

Cultivating a Tolerance for Ambiguity

Contrary to other scientific disciplines, the practice of psychology, and more specifically psychotherapy, lies within the terrain of both art and science. The various theories of human behavior and change provide assistance in understanding psychopathology. It has been a common practice to situate oneself within a particular school of psychotherapy and its concomitant theoretical base. This allows one to be grounded within a specific frame of thought and theoretical explanation for human behavior. At best, these types of theories serve to alleviate or defend against anxiety that inevitably arises when confronted with novel or ambiguous situations.

Alternatively, it is likely that there are several competing or complementary theoretical perspectives that one is faced with, or is actively integrating during the initial stages of learning psychotherapy, or throughout one's professional career. It may be a more helpful practice to cultivate a tolerance for ambiguity, to learn to broaden one's ability to deal with ambiguous or even competing information. Another way of understanding this is to consciously confront and make peace with the anxiety that emerges when one does not know the *right answer* since this alleged right answer seldom exists. "Try to love the questions themselves" (Rilke, 1984, p. 35) is perhaps a more appropriate framework for these issues. More realistically, gradients of good answers or responses exist on a continuum. Welcoming this framework of not knowing can open doors of possibilities, responses, and actions. This is clearly a fitting dimension of ethical decision making.

PART TWO: ETHICAL AND LEGAL ISSUES

Prominent and highly referenced ethical and legal issues integral to the practice of psychotherapy are presented within Part Two. Studying these will provide a foundational understanding of the ethical framework embodied within psychotherapeutic practice. Seasoned practitioners will find these issues merit revisiting and will contribute to an ongoing integration process. The most salient characteristics of particular issues are highlighted within quick reference frames contained throughout the section.

This monograph contains a compendium of laws and ethical issues that affect therapists. While ethical codes remain somewhat constant and are periodically updated by professional associations, laws evolve more frequently. New legislative bills are continually introduced and laws are reinterpreted or clarified based on appellate or supreme court decisions. With this in mind, my intention has been to create an accurate and professionally relevant work, focusing on a selection of laws and ethical issues central to the practice of psychotherapy.

Practicing ethically requires a familiarity with the relevant laws affecting the practice of psychotherapy. Informative laws can be found in the following codes in California: Business and Professions Code, Civil Code, Insurance Code, Health and Safety Code, Family Code, California Code of Regulations, Title 15 and 16, and Penal Code. The following website is helpful for viewing the text of these codes: <www.leginfo.ca.gov> Please consult with an attorney familiar with case law and the practice of psychotherapy, when seeking the most accurate and up to date information on the legal parameters.

Ethical standards and aspirational goals are promulgated by professional associations such as the American Psychological Association and California Association for Marriage and Family Therapists. Copies of these ethical standards are located in the Appendix for your reference. The following ethical and legal guidelines will serve to assist you in attaining acceptable standards of practice. Of course many psychotherapists attempt to attain the highest standards in their work, and this volume will also support you in this endeavor.

ADULT ABUSE: Dependent Adult and Elder Abuse

All states have mandated reporting requirements for suspected cases of child abuse or neglect. Most states have similar reporting laws for abuse or neglect of the elderly and dependent adult. The California reporting laws for child abuse and dependent adult and elder abuse are quite similar. Psychotherapists with limited experience in reporting these different types of victimization and those interested in learning more may contact the adult protective services department in their communities, an elder adult care ombudsperson, professional associations regarding training in recognizing abuse, and refer to the Welfare and Institutions Code Section 15610.

The new Elder/Dependent Adult Abuse Reporting Law became effective on January 1, 1999, in California: Welfare and Institutions Code beginning with Section 15610. Under this new law, therapists are mandated to report certain forms of abuse which were previously considered optional. The categories of physical abuse, neglect, abandonment, isolation, and financial abuse (formerly termed fiduciary abuse) require mandated reports. These changes came about after the Governor signed Senate Bill 2199 and Assembly Bill 1780 in September of 1998.

Legal Standard

When a therapist, "in his or her professional capacity, or within the scope of his or her employment, has observed or has knowledge of an incident that reasonably appears to be physical abuse, abandonment, isolation, financial abuse, or neglect, or is told by an elder or dependent adult that he or she has experienced behavior constituting physical abuse, abandonment, isolation, financial abuse, or neglect, or reasonably suspects abuse shall report the known or suspected instance of abuse by telephone immediately or as so as practically possible, and by written report sent within two working days" (Welfare and Institutions Code §15630). The therapist is required to report that abuse to an adult protective agency, often contained within the social services department of the county.

This new standard is similar (but not identical) to the current child abuse reporting duty, in that reasonable suspicion is now included. Previously abuse fitting within the categories of abandonment, isolation, financial abuse, and neglect was not mandated since the law required that the incident of abuse was either observed by the therapist or that the elder told the therapist about the abuse. As an example, it is now clear that when a perpetrator tells a mandated reporter, such as a therapist, that he or she physically abused an elder or dependent adult, the therapist is mandated to report.

Mandated Reports

A known or reasonably suspected case of physical abuse (injury inflicted by other than accidental means), abandonment, isolation, financial abuse, or neglect involving a dependent adult or elderly person must be reported. A telephone report must be made immediately or as soon as practically possible followed up by a written report within two working days. Immunity exists for civil and criminal liability for mandated reports.

Mandated Report
Dependent Adult and Elder Abuse
Mandated Reports

1. Phone Immediately - to the adult protective service agency;
2. Written Report within Two Working Days

Optional Reports

Reports are optional, not mandated, if the therapist reasonably suspects or has knowledge of types of elder or dependent adult abuse that are not mandated, such that his or her emotional well-being is endangered in any way. The law does not specify what these categories of abuse may be.

Dependent Adult

As per Welfare and Institutions Code §15610, a dependent adult is a "Person . . . between 18 and 64 who has physical or mental limitations that restrict his or her ability to carry out normal activities or to protect his or her rights including, but not limited to, persons who have physical or developmental disabilities or whose physical or mental abilities have diminished because of age." The definition of dependent adult includes persons who are between this age range and are admitted as an inpatient to a 24-hour facility, as defined in the Health and Safety Code Sections 1250, 1250.2, and 1250.3.

Elderly Adult

An elderly adult is defined as an individual age 65 or older.

Physical Abuse

Assault, battery, assault with a deadly weapon, unreasonable physical restraint, prolonged or continual deprivation of food or water, or sexual assault.*

*Sexual assault is sexual battery, rape, rape in concert, spousal rape, incest, sodomy, oral copulation or penetration of a genital or anal opening by a foreign object.

The definition of physical abuse encompasses the following: the use of "physical or chemical restraint or psychotropic medication:

a) for punishment;
b) for a period beyond that for which the medication was ordered pursuant to the instructions of a California-licensed physician and surgeon, who is providing medical care to the elder or dependent adult at the time the instructions are given; or
c) for any purpose not authorized by the physician and surgeon" (WIC §15610).

Neglect

This term includes "the negligent failure of any person having the care or custody of an elder or a dependent adult to exercise that degree of care that a reasonable person in a like position would exercise." This includes a failure to assist in personal hygiene, failure to provide for medical care (for physical and mental health needs), and failure to prevent malnutrition or dehydration.

Self-neglect is now reportable under this new law. The bill responsible for this legislation included historical information on the severity of this problem, referring to the 225,000 incidents annually (of elder or dependent adult abuse in California), and highlighted the fact that in more than fifty percent of all incidents, the adult is unable to meet his or her own needs due to frailty, untreated health conditions, mental or emotional problems, or family dysfunctions.

Abandonment

Abandonment is defined as desertion or willful forsaking by anyone having care or custody of an elder or dependent adult. An essential element within the definition is the provision that this is considered under the circumstance in which a reasonable person would continue to provide care and custody.

Isolation

Isolation is defined as fitting into four specific categories, however, if a physician providing care for the dependent or elder adult gives these as medical instructions (as part of the medical care) it is not:

a) acts intentionally committed to prevent an adult from receiving mail or phone calls,
b) falsely telling a caller or visitor that the adult does not wish to speak or meet with the individual, and this is done to prevent contact with family, friends, or others,
c) false imprisonment,
d) physical restraint, for the purposes of preventing the adult from meeting with visitors.

Financial Abuse

Financial abuse is the new term, and occurs in situations where one or both of the following circumstances exist:

a) When a person takes, secretes, or appropriates an elder or dependent adult's money or property, to any wrongful use, or with the intend to defraud, or
b) When a dependent adult or an elder (who would be considered dependent if between the ages of 18 and 64) <u>requests</u> a transfer of property or funds and <u>a third party does not take reasonable steps</u> to follow through and <u>acts in bad faith</u>.

Elder Abuse and Dependent Adult Abuse

- Physical Abuse
- Neglect
- Abandonment
- Isolation
- Financial Abuse

The American Psychiatric Association proposed a limitation on the duty to report elder abuse or dependent adult abuse that currently serves as a safeguard. The therapist is not required to make a report when the elder or dependent adult tells of the abuse, abandonment, isolation, financial abuse, or neglect, and; the therapist is not aware of any independent corroborating evidence, and; the elder or dependent adult has been diagnosed with a mental illness, defect, dementia, or incapacity, and; the therapist reasonably believes that the abuse did not occur. Note: please remember that this does not impose a duty on the therapist to investigate a known or suspected incident of abuse. Investigations are the responsibility of the adult protective services department.

In addition to the mandated duty to report, safety concerns for this population must be addressed whether the patient is a victim of abuse, neglect, abandonment, or financial abuse. In some instances in order to ameliorate the abuse, difficult and stressful changes in the environment may occur, such as a change in primary caretaker, residential facility, or skilled nursing home with assisted living programs. The skilled clinician is aware of the potential consequences of such changes, including the potential losses the adult may experience. Capacity or competency assessments may need to be made and perhaps a guardian appointed. As a psychotherapist, working from a team approach with other professionals will assist you in your work with the elderly and dependent adult population. Referrals may include physicians, psychologists, social workers, marriage and family therapists, elderly care ombudspersons, adult protective services, and in-home health care. For this reason it is important to become familiar with the resources and the specialists available within your community.

ADVERTISING

Psychotherapists may engage in informational activities to enable individuals to choose psychotherapeutic services. Several professional organizations (American Psychological Association, California Association for Marriage and Family Therapists) set forth standards for proper advertising and promotional activities. The provisions and interpretations are summarized below. See appendix for the full version of both ethical codes.

Accurate and truthful representation of relevant competence, education, training, and experience; only claiming a specialization if related training, education and supervised experience meet recognized professional standards; not misrepresenting qualifications of trainees, interns, or other associates. Psychotherapists are also responsible for information that appears within an advertisement and should take appropriate action to make clarifications or corrections when necessary.

Advertisements are crafted to furnish sufficient and clear information for the public to make an appropriate selection. This may include name, address, telephone number, fee structure, relevant degrees, state licenses, description of specialty or practice, and professional association membership. If you use the term psychotherapist to describe your practice, include either the full name of your licensure or license number (California Code of Regulations Title 16, § 1811), since the professions of marriage and family therapy, psychology, and social work may all practice psychotherapy. Omitting this information is considered misleading.

Inappropriate conduct includes using a false or misleading business name; making false public statements; making any claim or statement that is false, misleading, or deceptive, or encouraging or allowing patients to have false or exaggerated expectations regarding the services offered. If you are a therapist in training, your advertisements should indicate this along with your supervisor's name and license number.

Advertising

- Advertising is Permitted
- Accurate & Truthful Representation
- Sufficient & Clear Information

CHILD ABUSE

Ethical and Legal Issues

A variety of professional responsibilities and liabilities are associated with protecting children from abuse and neglect. As a licensed psychotherapist or a psychotherapist in training, you have an ethical and legal obligation to report suspected child maltreatment, generally referred to as child abuse. Once you have a reasonable suspicion of child abuse, a telephone report is made immediately or as soon as practically possible, followed by a written report within 36 hours. Every state has statutes categorizing child abuse as a crime, providing definitions for all terms and establishing punishments.

The primary purpose of the law is to protect children from abuse and to "ensure the safety, protection and physical and emotional well-being of children who are at risk of that harm. This safety, protection, and physical and emotional well-being may include provision of a full array of social and health services to help the child and family and to prevent reabuse of children. The focus shall be on the preservation of the family as well as the safety, protection, and physical and emotional well-being of the child" (Welfare and Institutions Code § 300.2). Children and family members are often referred to counseling and psychological treatment.

There are three sources for laws relevant to child abuse and protection: statutes, regulations (from executive branch of government), and court decisions. For example, Congress passed the Child Abuse Prevention and Treatment Act in 1974. The National Center on Child Abuse and Neglect emerged from this Act. NCCAN publishes manuals to provide guidance to professionals involved in the child protection system and to nurture community collaboration and quality of service delivery. This agency also provides federal funding for research in child abuse including prevention and treatment.

Therapists in California are required to have a basic understanding of child abuse, including assessment and reporting, and how one develops a reasonable suspicion of child maltreatment. Reasonable suspicion is based on your education, training, and experience. Once you have a reasonable suspicion you are expected to follow through with the procedure for making an appropriate report. After a report is made to the appropriate child protective services agency, an investigation is often conducted.

The following overview provides legal standards and definitions of child maltreatment including physical abuse, sexual abuse, neglect, and willful cruelty, mandated reporting discernment, assessment of reasonable suspicion including child and parental indicators, and concludes with initial clinical interventions. These elements will assist you in formulating your response to a child abuse disclosure and the proximal events surrounding a child maltreatment report.

CHILD ABUSE: Legal Standards

Child Abuse - California Penal Code Definition

"Child abuse means a physical injury which is inflicted by other than accidental means on a child by another person . . . the sexual abuse of a child . . . willful cruelty or unjustifiable punishment of a child . . . unlawful corporal punishment or injury . . . or neglect of a child or abuse in out-of-home care. Child abuse does not mean a mutual affray between minors" (Penal Code §11165.6).

Child Maltreatment - Federal Definition

The physical or mental injury, sexual abuse or exploitation, negligent treatment, or maltreatment of a child by a person who is responsible for the child's welfare under circumstances which indicate harm or threatened harm to the child's health or welfare. This definition is drawn from the Federal

Child Abuse Prevention and Treatment Act. 42 United States Code 5106g(4). See also, 45 C.F.R. 1340.2(d). Child maltreatment includes child abuse and child neglect. Definitions specific to a particular state will generally be found in one or more of its civil or criminal statutes.

Reporting Guideline

"Any health practitioner . . . who has knowledge of or observes a child in his or her professional capacity or within the scope of his or her employment whom he or she knows or reasonably suspects has been the victim of child abuse shall report the known or suspected instance of child abuse to a child protective agency immediately or as soon as practically possible by telephone and shall prepare and send a written report thereof within 36 hours of receiving the information concerning the incident" (Penal Code § 11166).

Confidentiality of Report

The identity of the mandated reporter and the contents of the report are legally confidential, disclosable only to child protective agencies, designated counsel, by court order, or when the mandated reporter has waived confidentiality.

Reasonable Suspicion

Reasonable suspicion means that it is objectively reasonable for a person to entertain such a suspicion, based upon facts that could cause a reasonable person in a like position, drawing on his or her training and experience, to suspect child abuse. The pregnancy of a minor does not, in and of itself, constitute the basis of reasonable suspicion of sexual abuse.

Child

A person under the age of 18.

Physical Abuse

Physical injury inflicted by other than accidental means on a child by another person. Examples: Bruises, cuts, scratches, scars, burns, fractures, central nervous system injuries, life-threatening abuse. Does not include results of mutual affray among minors, i.e., injuries caused by two children fighting by mutual consent (Penal Code §11165.6). Common signs of physical abuse are injuries at various stages of healing, burns, bruises, and bleeding.

Sexual Abuse

The laws on sexual abuse are fairly clear. However, be mindful of the issues noted below on consensual intercourse and the reporting requirements. Sexual abuse is legally defined as:

Rape and rape in concert; incest; sodomy; lewd and lascivious acts* upon a child under the age of 14, i.e., adult exposing him or herself or masturbating in front of a child; oral copulation, penetration of a genital or anal opening by a foreign object; or child molestation i.e., fondling sexually.

*Since January 1, 1998, the crime of lewd and lascivious acts with a minor has been clarified, and such conduct is reportable: where a person commits a lewd or lascivious act upon or with a victim who is a child of 14 or 15 years, where the person committing the act is at least 10 years older than the child/victim. (Lewd and lascivious is generally defined and interpreted by the courts as causing any touching of a child by the perpetrator or by the child at the direction of the perpetrator for the purpose of arousing, appealing to or gratifying the lust, or the passions, or the sexual desires of the person or the child). This kind of conduct had been reportable for many years, but only when the minor was under 14. It has been expanded to include 14 and 15 year olds.

Minor Engaging in a Consensual Sexual Relationship

If the minor is under 14, a report would be required, unless the minor's partner is also under 14 (keep in mind similar ages, not disparate age difference, for example two 13 year olds engaging in consensual sex). If the minor is 14 or over, a report would not be mandated, assuming no coercion at all is involved - with the exception noted below (effective January 1, 1998). In situations in which a report is not mandated, or you are not sure if one is mandated, reach out for consultation, e.g., call the child protective services agency for consultation.

*As of January 1, 1998, one subdivision of the unlawful sexual intercourse statute became reportable (as a result of Assembly Bill 327 - Havice). That subdivision (d) deals with the circumstance where any person 21 years or older engages in an act of sexual intercourse with a minor who is under 16 years of age. Thus, if a minor is under 16 engaging in sexual intercourse with a person 21 or older, this is a mandated reporting situation.

Planned Parenthood Affiliates v. Van de Kamp (181 California Appellate Court 3d 245)

The following refers to minors over 14 engaging in consensual sexual relationships. This California Court of Appeals ruling held that "a fundamental part of the [child abuse] reporting law is to allow the trained professional to distinguish an abusive and non-abusive situation. Instead of a blanket reporting requirement of all activity of those under a certain age, the professional can make a judgment as to whether the minor is having voluntary relations or being abused." Thus, professionals are expected to use their judgment in these instances.

The following clarification refers to minors under 14 years of age engaging in consensual intercourse.

In trying to ascertain the spirit and intent of the child abuse reporting laws, the appellate court wrote their provisions: "contemplate criminal acts of child abuse causing trauma to the victim, and do not contemplate the voluntary sexual associations between young children under the age of 14 who are not victims of a child abuser and are not the subjects of sexual victimization."

Sexual Exploitation

Conduct involving matter depicting a minor engaging in obscene acts, including promoting, aiding or assisting, using, persuading, inducing or coercing a child to engage in prostitution or pornography. Employing, permitting, or encouraging minors to engage in conduct depicting obscene sexual acts, such as live performances, posing, modeling, acting in video/ films, or prostitution.

Adults Abused as Minors

In such situations, a report of the abuse experienced by the patient is not mandated. However, if you find that you have acquired a reasonable suspicion of current abuse, i.e., that your patient's abuser is currently victimizing other children, you would be mandated to file a child abuse report. Based on the Informal Opinion of the California Attorney General, published February 3, 1987, the intention of the law is to protect children.

Willful Cruelty or Unjustifiable Punishment of a Child

Contributing to infliction of unjustifiable physical pain or mental suffering which endangers the child's person or health. A situation where any person willfully causes or permits any child to suffer, or inflicts thereon, unjustifiable physical pain or mental suffering such that his or her person or health is endangered.

Unlawful Corporal Punishment or Injury

Willfully inflicted punishment or injury to a child that results in a traumatic condition. A situation where any person willfully inflicts upon any child any cruel or inhuman corporal punishment or injury resulting in a traumatic condition.

Neglect

Severe Neglect:

Negligent failure of a person having the care or custody of a child to protect child from severe malnutrition or medically diagnosed non organic failure to thrive; willfully causing or permitting the child's person or health to be endangered by failure to provide adequate food, clothing, shelter, or medical care.

General Neglect

Negligent failure of a person having the care or custody of a child to provide child with adequate food, clothing, shelter, medical care, or supervision where no physical injury has occurred. Does not include leaving child unsupervised under reasonable circumstances.

Immunity

The mandated reporter is provided with immunity from criminal and civil liability for reporting as required (report must be in "good faith"), and can receive up to $50,000 for reimbursement of attorney's fees necessary to defend against a civil action brought on the basis of the report.

CHILD ABUSE: Mandated Reporting Discernment

Mandated Reporting

It is essential to meet any reporting obligations (by phone immediately or as soon as practically possible: in writing within 36 hours) if you acquire a reasonable suspicion of child abuse in your professional capacity. You are not obligated to tell your patient of the report, but it is usually in the best interests of the patient and the therapeutic relationship if this information is not withheld. Adjust your treatment plan to address the abuse and refer to another therapist if the therapeutic relationship is irreparably damaged.

Telephone report: The phone report of a known or suspected instance of child abuse includes your name, the child's name and present location, the nature and extent of injury, and any information that led you to suspect child abuse.

Written report: The written reports are submitted on forms adopted by the Department of Justice, and includes a narrative description, a summary of what the abused child or person accompanying the child said, and information on any known history of similar incidents for the child.

Reasonable Suspicion Assessment

Reasonable Suspicion.

Remember that reasonable suspicion means it is objectively reasonable for a person to entertain such a suspicion and that training and experience is drawn upon. The process of developing reasonable suspicion of child abuse often involves the visual signs and behaviors seen by the psychotherapist, such as physical marks in cases of physical abuse. The behavior of parents may provide important information, leading to the overall development of reasonable suspicion. The psychotherapist may have the opportunity to observe the parent-child interactions, which provide helpful diagnostic information about the interpersonal relationship as well.

The following categories and indicators are listed to assist in the process of developing reasonable suspicion. Although the indicators are correlated with child abuse, they may or may not be indicative of child abuse in the specific instance you are assessing. Reasonable suspicion is preferably derived from the presence of multiple factors and the interpretation of these factors based on one's education, training, and experience. At a minimum, when these indicators appear, your curiosity will be engaged and you will want to know more information. Becoming familiar with the literature on child abuse will prove helpful. This next section shows how the child abuse literature assists us in understanding the indicators of child abuse.

A body of extensive literature exists on parental or perpetrator characteristics (Milner, 1991; Milner & Chilamkurti,

1991). One significant finding indicates that although a percentage of abused children become abusive parents, estimated at 30%, (Kaufman & Zigler, 1987), most of them do not become abusers (Widom, 1989). Many of these characteristics reflect high levels of distress or dysfunction and inappropriate parenting strategies (Factor & Wolfe, 1990). Behaviorally, parents have been found to exhibit inconsistent child-rearing practices that reflect critical, hostile, or aggressive styles (Trickett & Kuczynski, 1986). Cognitively, abusive parents tend to hold negative attributions toward their children's behavior or tend to perceive their children in negative ways (Azar & Siegel, 1990). Abusive parents may exhibit little attention to their children or express limited positive affect and behavior toward them (Caliso & Milner, 1992; Kavanaugh, Youngblood, Reid, & Fagot, 1988).

Parental Clues to Assess for Signs of Abuse

- Parent may be unable to describe positive characteristics of child;
- Perceives child in negative manner;
- Limited attention expressed to the child;
- Inappropriate parenting strategies, e.g., harsh and rigid;
- Critical, hostile, or aggressive style;
- Unrealistic expectations of the child (e.g., toilet-training a 6 month-old child);
- May turn to child to have his or her own needs met.
- Parental explanation for the child abuse injury or symptom clearly does not fit the injury.

Behavioral Indicators in the Child

These should serve only as warning signals to look further. The information on behavioral indices and symptoms is primarily derived from the literature focusing on clinical samples, unlike adult samples, where studies have been conducted with nonclinical and clinical samples for comparison.

Physical Abuse - Behavioral Indices:
- Child exhibits sudden changes in behavior or mood, e.g,, extreme fear or withdrawn behavior around others; overly compliant; or sudden changes with peers.
- may be hypervigilant, depressed, underactive;
- may become accident prone or engage in self injurious behavior (e.g,, cutting)
- exhibits unmanageable (for child) behaviors (rageful, panics, easily agitated);

Neglect:
A child who has been physically neglected may show observable signs of gross malnourishment, failure to thrive, or developmental delays (Crittenden & Ainsworth, 1989) but most types of neglect leave no physical marks. Behaviorally, the child may engage in avoidant behavior, may isolate self, or interact less with peers than other non-neglected children (Hoffman-Plotkin & Twentyman, 1984); may be depressed or passive, may seem uninterested in soliciting care and warmth from caretakers or teachers.

Neglect:- Behavioral Indices
- gross malnourishment;
- failure to thrive;
- developmental delays
- avoidant behavior; isolates self; interacts less with peers
- depressed or passive
- uninterested in soliciting care or warmth

Emotional Abuse:
Child may not seek comfort when distressed (Crittenden & Ainsworth, 1989); frequent self-denigrating comments; behavioral problems in school such as aggression or disruptions (Hart & Brassard, 1991); reduced emotional responsiveness, low self-esteem, negative self-concept (Rohner & Rohner, 1980; Shengold, 1979).

Emotional Abuse - Behavioral Indices:

- May not seek comfort when distressed
- Self-denigrating comments
- Behavioral problems, aggressive or disruptive
- Reduced emotional responsiveness
- Low self-esteem
- Negative self-concept

Sexual Abuse:
Child may exhibit increased sexual behavior (Friedrich, Grambsch, Broughton, Kuiper, & Beilke, 1991; Gil & Johnson, 1993); may exhibit suicidal behavior (Lanktree, Briere, & Zaidi, 1991) may develop eating disorders; alcohol or other substance abuse problems (Singer, Petchers, & Hussey, 1989); may run away or be truant (Hibbard, Ingersoll, & Orr, 1990); may exhibit fear, anxiety, and concentration problems (Conte & Schuerman, 1987); engage in self injurious behaviors, such as cutting, burning, pulling out hair (van der Kolk, Perry, & Herman, 1991).

Sexual Abuse - Behavioral Indices

- Increased sexual behavior
- Suicidal behavior
- Alcohol or other substance abuse
- Runs away or is truant
- Fear, Anxiety, Concentration problems
- Self injurious behaviors

CHILD ABUSE: Initial Interventions

1. Safety of the Child.

Assess the current safety of the child and the other children in the home. Maintain an unbiased attitude, avoiding words, gestures, and facial expressions that express or suggest shock and disapproval. Remember the importance of neutrality and eschew any accusatory, blaming, or interpretive statements.

2. Legally Mandated Reporting Requirement.

When reasonable suspicion has been acquired, report immediately by telephone and within 36 hours in writing to a child protective services agency or law enforcement.

3. Current Crisis.

If you have the opportunity, clarify precipitating events to this crisis. Focus on the welfare of the child and the parents. Remember that shame, guilt, distress, feelings of helplessness, and rage may be experienced. Use open-ended questions, such as "How did this occur?" rather than "Did you do this to the child?" Depending on the circumstances, a physician referral may be considered for a physical examination to assess the patient for any physical damage caused by the abuse and receive treatment if necessary. Avoid condoning the parents' or caretakers' behaviors. Use statements acknowledging the feelings or thoughts, such as "I see that you were very angry" rather than "Any parent would have felt the same way in that situation." Provide information about the reporting process, the role of child protective services, and the courts. Attempt to reduce shame in the victim by emphasizing that it was good to come forward and make the disclosure.

Assist the victim and family members clarify their thoughts and feelings through the process of stating responses and labeling feelings. Provide emotional support through encouragement and empathic listening. Convey concern and willingness to help alleviate stress.

4. Social Support.

Assist the family to mobilize their support network. Helpful referrals and adjunctive services include self-help groups, such as Parents Anonymous, Parents United, Adults Molested as Children United, Daughters and Sons United, hotlines, day care. Some social services programs such as in-home care, may reduce environmental stressors that interfere with effective parenting.

Depending on the issues at hand: help the family develop appropriate coping and parenting skills. Identify and develop strategies such as parenting skills, perhaps refer to educational programs such as anger management, Parent Effectiveness Training, Systematic Training for Effective parenting. Structured programs often focus on education, child development, the acquisition of cognitive behavioral strategies in dealing with parenting issues. The integration of new problem solving methods in addition to relaxation training may be helpful.

Child Abuse Resources

The American Professional Society on the Abuse of Children (See Appendix A) is an interdisciplinary organization devoted to child abuse treatment and prevention. The organization engages in advocacy and provides information, guidelines, and referral services to professionals working in the field. Practice guidelines are available on conducting psycho-social evaluations of children, sexual abuse assessments, and psychological maltreatment.

Child Abuse Initial Interventions

- Safety of the Child
- Mandated Reporting
- Focus on Current Crisis
- Engage Social Support

CHILD CUSTODY EVALUATIONS

Child custody evaluations are conducted when a suitable child custody arrangement cannot be agreed to by divorcing parents or parents who wish to restructure parental rights and responsibilities. The courts may modify custody and visitation rights until the children are 18 years of age. If you provide or provided psychotherapeutic services to a member of a family contemplating a child custody evaluation, it is considered inappropriate to function as an expert witness i.e., the child custody evaluator, for this particular family. However, it is likely that you would be interviewed or called to testify as a fact witness within this case regarding information you became aware of during the psychotherapeutic relationship.

Evidence code §730 states:

When it appears to the court, at any time before or during the trial of an action, that expert evidence is or may be required by the court or a party to the action, the court on its own motion or on motion of any party may appoint one or more experts to investigate, to render a report as may be ordered by the court, and to testify as an expert at the trial of the action relative to the fact or matter as to which the expert evidence is or may be required."

Qualified persons who conduct child custody evaluations include licensed marriage and family therapists, licensed clinical social workers, and psychologists. Psychological testing is often conducted and if the child custody evaluator is not qualified to administer and interpret the results, a referral to a qualified individual is made. Usually a minimum of a master's degree in a mental health field is required, with the additional training and knowledge of issues such as child development, divorce, and the legal standards and process involved in these matters. Competence to conduct an evaluation involves one's professional education, training, experience, and/or supervision.

When conducting an evaluation, the child's or children's best psychological interests are paramount. The evaluator is functioning as an expert witness, not as a psychotherapist or mediator. An expert witness is required to be neutral and non-discriminatory, focused on the parental capacity of each parent, and the psychological development and needs of the child. Data gathering techniques include history taking, clinical interviews with each parent and child separately and together, first hand observations in the office and home, psychological assessments, and ancillary information, such as pertinent knowledge from teachers, colleagues, relatives, and neighbors. If it is deemed appropriate and the child is mature enough, i.e., sufficient age and capacity to state a preference, the court will also consider the child's wishes.

An evaluation often results in a professional opinion containing a recommendation in the best interests of the child or children. Since the ultimate issue is actually decided by the judge, another way of understanding 730 evaluations, is that the expert witness assists the Superior Court Judge in making a decision as to the best custodial arrangement.

One last note regarding joint custody versus sole custody. In studies conducted by Ackerman and Ackerman (1997), experienced professionals indicated they preferred joint custody with primary placement with one parent or joint custody with shared placement. A less preferred child custody arrangement was reported to be sole custody with visitation privileges. Although a form of joint custody may be preferred, in high conflict or hostile and violent families, sole custody by one parent, with visitation privileges by the other may be the best possible arrangement. Many variables are weighed, including history of domestic violence, the amount of hostility, anger, and bitterness between the parents, willingness of the parents to enter into a joint custodial agreement, substance abuse, parenting skills and behaviors, move away issues, quality of the parent-child relationship, and psychological stability.

In terms of domestic violence during dissolution of marriage, Johnston and Campbell (1993) reported five basic types of interpersonal violence seen within custody disputes and the resulting impact on the children: ongoing or episodic male battering, female-initiated violence, male-controlling interactive violence, separation-engendered violence or postdivorce trauma, and psychotic and paranoid reactions. They recommended against sole or joint custody for a father who is involved in ongoing or episodic battering, and against sole or joint custody for a parent who is psychotic or has paranoid delusions. The safety of the children was of the utmost importance.

For more information on professional guidelines in conducting child custody evaluations, please refer to the American Psychological Association's Guidelines for Child Custody Evaluations in Divorce Proceedings (1994) and the Standards of Practice for Child Custody Evaluations promulgated by the Association of Family and Conciliation Courts (1995).

CONCURRENT TREATMENT FROM OTHER THERAPISTS

The intention is to act in accordance with the best interests of the patient. Depending on the circumstances, it may or may not be unethical to see a patient who is concurrently seeing one or more other therapists. A therapist should carefully consider the treatment issues and the potential patient's welfare. The therapist discusses these issues with the patient in order to minimize the risk of confusion and conflict, consults with the other therapists when appropriate, and proceeds with caution and sensitivity to the therapeutic issues.

If a patient is concurrently seeing one or more therapists, and it is determined that therapy with you is in the patient's best interests, you may proceed with the therapy. Some examples include: The patient is in individual therapy with you and in couple's therapy with another provider, or is receiving issue specific therapy (e.g. systematic desensitization for a phobia) elsewhere outside the scope of your training or experience.

If a patient is in concurrent therapy with another therapist and appears to be hiding this fact from his or her other therapist perhaps as a way of defending against benefiting from therapy, it would be unethical for you to continue seeing this patient if there was no apparent therapeutic benefit.

Concurrent Treatment

- Assess the Situation
- Discuss with Patient
- Consult with Other Therapist

CONFIDENTIALITY

The ethical and legal responsibility to maintain the confidentiality of patient-psychotherapist communications, including the fact that a particular person is or is not a patient, is essential both to the effectiveness of therapy and the patient's safety and well-being. Confidentiality is considered a foundational and necessary element in psychotherapy, and builds on the right of privacy, going "beyond that afforded by the federal constitution" (Caudill & Pope, 1995, p. 166). Professional associations, licensing boards, and legal statutes all provide severe consequences for unauthorized disclosures, such as disciplinary action, expulsion from professional membership (Mills, 1984), censure, reprimand (Hall & Hare-Mustin, 1983), revocation of license to practice, and civil or criminal penalties. The ultimate consequence is the betrayal perpetrated by the therapist upon the patient.

Information disclosed by a patient to a psychotherapist, covered by the psychotherapist-patient privilege, is considered confidential. However, since privilege is established by statute and case law, some communications are not privileged. *Refer to the section on Privilege within this text for further information on the limitations of the scope of privilege.

Confidential communication between patient and psychotherapist is defined in Evidence Code Section 1012. The following is an excerpt: "information obtained by an examination of the patient, transmitted between a patient and his psychotherapist in the course of that relationship and in confidence by a means which, so far as the patient is aware, discloses the information to no third persons other than those who are present to further the interest of the patient in the consultation, or those to whom disclosure is reasonably necessary for the transmission of the information or the accomplishment of the purpose for which the psychotherapist is consulted, and includes a diagnosis made and the advice given by the psychotherapist in the course of that relationship." Even with the legally permitted consultation noted in the last part of this definition, it is considered sensible ethical practice to obtain a written consent from the patient, delineating the specific information that will be shared or sought. "Obtaining written consent helps promote clarity of communication between therapist and client in situations when misunderstandings can be disastrous" (Pope & Vasquez, 1998, p. 226).

Despite the validity of confidentiality as both an ethical and legal mandate, it is disregarded intentionally and unintentionally far too often. Pope & Bajt (1988) reported confidentiality was the most frequent intentional ethical and legal violation by participants in their national study. Pope, Tabachnick, & Keith-Spiegel (1987) reported over half of the respondents in their study unintentionally violated patient confidentiality.

Under most circumstances confidential information should not be released without the explicit written consent of the patient. However, in certain circumstances, confidentiality must be or may be breached. These circumstances are:

1) Those in which a therapist is legally mandated to breach confidentiality (must be breached), and

2) Those in which a therapist is legally permitted but not obligated to do so (may be breached).

In those cases where a mandate to disclose confidential information exists, an ethical and well educated psychotherapist remembers to disclose only to the extent required by law. This means providing the limited necessary information, but nothing more. For this reason, keeping abreast of the relevant statutes affecting the practice of psychotherapy is crucial. If you are in doubt about required or permissible breaches, seek consultation immediately, to protect both the patient and yourself. The intention is to minimize inadvertent and improper disclosure. "Willful, unauthorized communication of information received in professional confidence" (Business & Professions Code § 2960) is considered unprofessional conduct.

Situations in which confidentiality must be breached:

- Tarasoff - Duty to Warn - If in the course of therapy, a patient has communicated to the psychotherapist a serious threat of physical violence against a reasonably identifiable victim or victims, the therapist must make reasonable efforts to communicate the threat to the victim(s) and to a law enforcement agency (Tarasoff v Regents of the University of California, Civil Code 43.92) .

- Child Abuse Reporting - When a therapist, in his or her professional capacity, knows or reasonably suspects that a child is being abused, he or she is legally obligated to make a report to a child protective agency (Penal Code § 11166).

- Dependent Adult and Elder Abuse - When a therapist, in his or her professional capacity, has observed an incident that reasonably appears to be physical abuse, has observed a physical injury which indicates that there has been abuse, is told by an elder or dependent adult that abuse has occurred, or reasonably suspects dependent adult or elder abuse, the therapist is required to report that abuse to an adult protective agency (Welfare and Institutions Code § 15630).

- Court Orders: When a court has recognized an exception to privilege and ordered the release of records or a psychotherapist's testimony, the individual must release the records or appear for testimony.

- *Assault or abuse: There is no longer any law requiring psychotherapists to breach confidentiality in cases of spousal assault or abuse. For a brief period of time, it had been required, then repealed. However, it was limited to those working in a clinic, health facility, or physician's office.*

Confidentiality: Legal Mandate to Breach

- Tarasoff
- Mandated Reporting Situations, e.g, Child Abuse, Elder Adult Abuse, Dependent Adult Abuse
- Court Orders

Situations in Which Confidentiality May Be Breached (Breach is permissible)

- Patient is a Danger to Self, Others, or Property (with no third-party identifiable victim involved). As per Evidence Code Section 1024, when the psychotherapist has reasonable cause to believe that a person is in such mental or emotional condition as to be dangerous to her or "himself or to the person or property of another and that disclosure of the communication is necessary to prevent the threatened danger" (emphasis added), a breach of confidentiality is permitted e.g., calling the police, a friend, the Psychiatric Assessment Team. This may include threats of suicide. Please see section on Suicidal Ideation.

- Patient is Gravely Disabled due to a mental disorder. When a patient is not competent to take reasonably good care of herself or himself, (assessed in the areas of food, clothing, and shelter,) a therapist may ethically breach confidentiality if reasonably providing for the health and welfare of the patient (Welfare and Institutions Code 5150).

- Non-Mandated Elder or Dependent Adult Abuse Reporting. When the criteria for a mandated report are not met, a report is optional. The law does not currently specify what these categories of abuse may be, however, an important element is the elder or dependent adult's emotional well-being is endangered. Clearly this requires an evaluation of the situation based on one's professional judgment.

Before psychotherapy begins, it is wise to provide an office policies form or therapeutic contract as part of gaining informed consent, including a brief outline of situations in which confidentiality must and may be breached. Such a form can help to reduce the problems associated with mandated or optional breaches of confidentiality. Having a document such as this can prove invaluable if and when situations arise where confidentiality may or must be breached. The document may be reviewed during psychotherapy as well. This would also help you meet the ethical obligation of informing patients of the legal limits of confidentiality.

DANGEROUSNESS

Psychotherapists have a professional responsibility to protect other people from potentially dangerous patients and to protect patients from themselves. Therapists must know their responsibilities to warn and protect potential victims. The differential diagnosis process in evaluating dangerousness and violent behavior, includes evaluating for substance intoxication, schizophrenia and other psychoses, mood disorders such as bipolar disorder, impulse control disorder, antisocial personality disorder, and paranoid personality disorder. The following sections provide information relevant to patient dangerousness to self, others, and the therapist.

DANGEROUSNESS: Patient Dangerous to Self

Bellah v. Greenson: A California Court of Appeals ruling that the Tarasoff mandated "duty to warn" did not apply to cases of threatened suicide. However, this case did establish a legal duty to take reasonable steps to prevent a threatened suicide. These steps depend on one's assessment of the level of danger, and what is required to prevent the threatened suicide. These steps can include measures such as a "no-suicide" contract, increasing the frequency of sessions, mobilizing the patient's support system, notifying a family member, and/or instituting involuntary hospitalization under the provisions of

Welfare and Institutions Code § 5150. See Suicidal Ideation for more information on addressing this issue.

Evidence Code 1024: "There is no privilege . . . if the psychotherapist has reasonable cause to believe that the patient is in such mental or emotional condition as to be dangerous to himself or to the person or property of another and that disclosure of the communication is necessary to prevent the threatened danger."

DANGEROUSNESS: Patient Dangerous to Others

When a patient communicates a serious threat of physical violence against a reasonably identifiable victim, the therapist must operate as a reasonably prudent practitioner by making reasonable efforts to communicate the threat to the potential victim, **and** to a law enforcement agency. The prevention of the violence may involve hospitalization of the patient, specifically when the severity of the violent ideation is extreme such as homicidal ideation, the patient's coping resources are minimal, and the presence of various factors, including the particular diagnosis and the capacity to maintain a no-violence contract.

Voluntary hospitalization would be considered prior to the more restrictive involuntary hospitalization. The Welfare and Institutions Code § 5150 allows for the involuntary confinement of a person, who as a result of a mental disorder is a danger to others, for 72 hour treatment and evaluation.

When engaging in therapy with a patient who may be dangerous, it is wise to use appropriate self-protection measures and structure. Provide a supportive environment that allows for the alleviation of symptoms through psychotherapy (perhaps increased frequency of sessions), social support, and medications. Psychiatric referral for a medication evaluation may also be appropriate.

With a rageful patient who may not be imminently dangerous to another, helpful goals are to provide for safety, structure, containment, and stability so patient will not harm self or others; to teach anger management and stress management techniques; to uncover and work toward resolution of underlying issues. In other words, to clinically address the issues which may diffuse the explosive situation.

Suggested Interventions:

Review patient's history.

Review how anger was handled in patient's family of origin. Note how the patient has dealt with anger in the past. Does the patient currently wish to deal differently with anger? Indicators of the potential for violence may include angry demeanor, substance intoxication, abuse, or use, poor impulse control, agitation, poor judgment, frustration, and irritable mood.

Focus on cognitions.

Examine cognitive distortions or belief system, such as the use of mind reading; unrealistic exaggeration; irrational beliefs; investment in "shoulds", unrealistic expectations.

Create a no-violence contract.

Offer a no-violence contract to minimize the potential threat.

Utilize a structured behavioral approach with a focus on managing anger

a) Teach a time out technique and distraction methods.
b) Counting backwards from 100 or from 10
c) Educating about the cycle of violence phases:
    1) Tension building,
    2) Acute episode or violent outburst,
    3) Loving respite or honeymoon phase,
    back to 1) tension building, etc.
d) Identifying anger triggers and avoiding them, or not responding to them
e) Keeping anger journal or diary.

DANGEROUSNESS: Patient Dangerous to Therapist

Safety is an essential issue within psychotherapy, and the therapist's safety is integral in working with a patient who may be violent. If a patient is angry and irritable but not dangerous, the situation may be diffused by providing support or allowing for ventilation of feelings, in addition to setting limits on the parameters of behavior, i.e., acceptable vs. unacceptable behaviors.

Suggested Preventative Measures:

1. See patients when others are in office if danger is suspected - best not to see patient if you are alone in the office or building.
2. Have emergency phone numbers readily available.
3. Sit near the door, allow for patient's easy exit and never block the door.
4. Inquire about any weapons and request they be placed in the trunk of patient's vehicle.

Self-Protective Measures if Threatened:

1. Inform others in your office or center, arranging for their support.
2. Leave the door to the office open.
3. Set clear limits on unacceptable behavior and describe the consequences of violent behavior.
4. If necessary, excuse yourself and call for help (911).
5. Prepare for the possibility of defending yourself, i.e., disarming the person or fighting back.

Many county mental health departments or local agencies have courses in Managing Assaultive Behavior. These can be quite valuable in acquiring information on prevention and self protection including learning methods such as verbal interventions and paying attention to physical considerations.

DIVERSITY ISSUES

It's essential to seek to understand the complex role that cultural and human diversity plays in your work. In a sense, all therapeutic interactions and thus interventions are multicultural. We all bring our varying attitudes, beliefs, values, behaviors, and cultural and historical backgrounds to the psychotherapeutic relationship. An awareness of, sensitivity to, and responsiveness to individual and group differences allow psychotherapists to assess, treat, and refer their patients properly and ethically.

Being sensitive to individual differences within groups provides clinicians with rich contextual information about the individuals they threat. Appreciating the full context of a patient's life involves a degree of curiosity, attentiveness, and inquisitiveness. "Knowledge about cultural and socioeconomic contexts becomes the basis for informed inquiry rather than illusion of uniform group characteristics with which to stereotype the client" (Pope & Vasquez, 1998, p. 210). Your willingness to examine underlying assumptions, ethnocentric attitudes, and personal limitations, will assist you in working with other perspectives in a non-judgmental manner and will enhance your continual development and practice of appropriate, relevant, and sensitive interventions in working with diverse patients.

When differences of age, gender, ability or disability, race, ethnicity, national origin, geographic region, religion, sexual orientation, disability, language, or socioeconomic status significantly affect a psychotherapist's work concerning particular individuals or groups, the psychotherapist must obtain the training, experience, consultation, or supervision necessary to ensure the competence of services, or make appropriate referrals.

Psychotherapists must be aware of potential bias and attempt to identify situations in which specific interventions, assessment techniques, or norms may not be applicable. Assessment tools may require adjustment in administration or interpretation because of factors such as gender, religion, age, culture, race, ethnicity, language, national origin, sexual orientation, disability, or socioeconomic status. When deciding whether to use psychological tests, which particular tests to use, or how to interpret test results, you must use caution if the patient is from a background significantly different from the normative samples. For example, the widely used MMPI, Minnesota Multiphasic Personality Inventory, did not include African Americans, Native Americans, Hispanics, or Asian Americans in the original normative sample. Fortunately it has been revised. Many tests will yield misleading results if a person's group status is not considered. Norm-referenced tests may lack validity when used with individuals from groups which were not adequately represented in the test's normative sample.

Diversity Issues

- Sensitivity
- Responsiveness
- Examine Underlying Assumptions
- Acknowledge Cultural Differences
- Consider Cultural Factors and Within Group Differences
- Acknowledge Personal Limitations
- Seek Consultation and Education

EMERGENCY PHONE CALL

When you receive an emergency phone call, your response is formulated with the intent to promote safety and stability and bring adjunctive help into play appropriately. Also protect confidentiality to the extent feasible. The welfare of the patient is essential.

Suggested Interventions:

1. Remain calm. Clinically assess the severity of the crisis the patient is experiencing, and the patient's ability to care for him or herself. Assist the patient in developing a number of options in the interest of insuring safety, such as asking a friend to stay over, mobilizing a personal support network, making an appointment for the next day. Contacting a law enforcement agency or mobile crisis response team could be helpful as well, particularly if the crisis is severe and the patient may wish to or need to be hospitalized. This may be the course of action you'll need to follow through on, depending on the situation. See Suicidal Ideation.

2. Crisis intervention workers advise obtaining the phone number called from as soon as is practically possible. This permits the police to trace the call and respond to the scene to provide assistance and allows you to phone back if disconnected.

3. If someone other than the patient phones to provide information on a crisis your patient is experiencing, you are required to protect the patient's confidentiality to the extent feasible. Your assessment of the information received, along with your clinical judgment of the case, and level of concern will dictate what type of action you take.

Emergency Phone Call

- Remain Calm
- Problem Solve
- Develop Options
- Obtain Phone Number
- Protect Confidentiality

FACTORS IN TAKING A CASE

The decision to take a case is dependent upon several factors. For clarity, I will place these factors into two distinct categories: factors about the patient and factors about the psychotherapist. Assessing and evaluating these factors prior to initiating psychotherapy is best, but may not always be possible. At times these factors come into play during the treatment process and should be attended to properly at that time.

Factors about the Patient

The ethical intention is to provide psychotherapy to patients who are willing, legally suitable, capable of relating to the psychotherapeutic process, and are benefiting from the experience. Working with patients who are not is considered unethical. Most therapists begin from the assumption that anyone is a suitable patient for therapy, then rule out legal and ethical exceptions to this.

Willingness

1. Does the person want to be in therapy?
2. Do he or she refuse to cooperate in any meaningful way if they are court referred?

Legally Suitable

1. Is the patient suitable for psychotherapy in terms of age?
2. If the patient is a minor who would like to be seen without parental consent, does he or she meet the exception (see Mi-

nors)?
3. If not, have you sought out parental consent and received assent from the minor?

Capable of Relating to the Process of Psychotherapy

Communication

1. Are there any language or communication difficulties?
2. If your primary language is English and the patient's is not, how comprehensive is the patient's understanding of English (and how comprehensive is your understanding of the patient's language, e.g, Spanish, or sign language?)
3. Is the patient best served with a referral or the addition of an interpreter?

Capacity

1. Is the person gravely disabled and lacking reasonable capacity to understand psychotherapy?
2. Is he or she able to provide informed consent or assent to treatment?

Is the individual under the influence of drugs or alcohol at the time therapy is provided? Although psychotherapists have varying degrees of prohibitive policies or allowances regarding this issue, substantial intoxication may render an individual incapable of providing informed consent to psychotherapeutic treatment.

Perhaps an alternative treatment context should be considered, e.g., inpatient hospitalization, partial hospitalization program, residential treatment facility, alcohol/drug rehabilitation program, or intensive day treatment program.

Factor in Contintuing Treatment:

Is the patient appreciably benefiting from the therapy after a reasonable time and effort by the therapist?

Factors in Taking a Case
Patient Factors

- willingness
- legally suitable
- capacity

Factors about the Psychotherapist

The intention here is to provide psychotherapy within the scope of practice, training, and experience. Other factors include the appropriate use of clinical judgment and the impact of multiple relationships and countertransference responses.

Scope of Practice

1. Is the issue or the work within your scope of practice?
2. If the issue is not legally within your scope of practice, you refer to an appropriate professional.

Scope of Education, Training, or Experience

1. Is the issue within your scope of education, training, or experience?
2. Are you substantially skilled in treating this population, issue, family developmental stage, etc.?
3. If not, are you seeking sufficient adjunctive training, consultation, or supervision to assist you?

Multiple Relationships

1. Do you or have you had a previous relationship with this individual, couple, or family?
2. Are you significantly engaged in other relationships which could impair your objectivity or judgment in this case?
3. For example, if seeing a couple, and you are in business with one partner's uncle.

Countertransference

In becoming aware of the range of your countertransference reactions, you are unable to manage them sufficiently (even after seeking consultation or supervision) and they interfere with psychotherapy.

Factors in Taking a Case
Therapist Factors

- scope of practice
- scope of education, training, experience
- multiple relationships
- unmanageable countertransference

FEES

Several issues are involved with the concept of fees, including setting a fee, when to discuss the fee, insurance issues, and bill collecting. "When finances are brought up in the course of a psychologist's formal training, specific discussion of actual practices involving billing, collection, and third-party reimbursement are rarely mentioned" (Koocher & Keith-Spiegel, 1998, p. 234). The successful independent practice of psychotherapy requires the appropriate management of these issues. (Insurance issues are addressed in the Insurance section).

Fee Setting

As early as possible, the therapist and patient should reach an agreement specifying the compensation including the billing arrangement (preferably during first contact, e.g., telephone call or intake session) so patient may decide to proceed based on informed consent. If limitations to services can be anticipated because of limitations in financing, this is discussed with the patient as early as possible. One approach is to charge the prevailing rate in the community, and maintain some low cost hours for a few patients who either can't afford full fee, or who suffer financial difficulties during on-going therapy. In order to learn about the prevailing rate, consult with colleagues and your professional association regarding recent surveys on independent practice (California Association for Marriage and Family Therapists has helpful information divided into geographic regions).

When Fee Is Not Affordable

You are not legally or ethically compelled to see patients for free unless there are special circumstances such as a crisis situation which you see the patient through. Financial issues should not take precedence over a patient's welfare. It is improper to simply abandon an existing patient because she/he cannot pay your fee. If the patient is in crisis, it may be important to see the patient through the crisis before terminating. You may work out a mutually agreeable arrangement with the patient, such as meeting less frequently or for a lower fee. Provide potential or actual patient with low or no cost referrals if it is not feasible for you to be the therapist.

Non-Payment of Fees

You may not withhold records that are later requested solely because payment has not been received. The patient's welfare takes precedence over financial issues. In circumstances where the patient has not paid the agreed upon fee, a collection agency may be utilized after you have exhausted all other means of collection and the patient has been informed the account will be turned over to a collection agency. Only information relevant to collecting payment may be released in these instances.

Fees

Set fee as Early as Possible
Patient's Welfare takes Precedence over financial Issues

GRAVE DISABILITY

Patient is Gravely Disabled due to a mental disorder. When a patient is not competent to take reasonably good care of herself or himself, (assessed in the areas of food, clothing, and shelter,) a therapist may ethically breach confidentiality if reasonably providing for the health and welfare of the patient.

When a patient is believed to be a danger to others, or to himself or herself, or gravely disabled due to a mental disorder, the county may, upon probable cause, provide for an involuntary 72 hour hold for treatment and evaluation at an approved psychiatric health facility. This procedure may be invoked by a county designated person such as a member of a crisis team, a sheriff, a police officer, or a mental health professional. This procedure is authorized by California Welfare and Institutions Code Section 5150.

Arrange for hospitalization when a patient is gravely disabled due to some form of mental disorder (imminently suicidal, out of control due to psychosis, etc.). Voluntary hospitalization is preferable, however since the patient is gravely disabled involuntary hospitalization is often the best recourse.

INFORMED CONSENT

Many years ago, in the times of Hippocrates, health practitioners were advised to conceal procedures from the patient. "Perform all this calmly and adroitly, concealing most things from the patient while you are attending to him" (as cited in O'Neill, 1998, p.10). Fortunately, the times have changed in favor of patients' rights. Thus the current standard emphasizes the affirmative duty of the psychotherapist to inform the patient about the treatment process including the possible shortcomings and risks.

Informed consent took seed in the Salgo v. Stanford University (1957) case in which the phrase was coined. Since that time many cases have brought further clarity to this concept. Currently, the widely accepted procedure is threefold:

1) provide the patient with significant information concerning psychotherapy (provided the patient has the capacity to consent),
2) obtain the patient's freely expressed consent, and
3) document the consent in the patient record.

If the patient is not legally capable of giving informed consent, the practitioner should provide information about the "proposed interventions in a manner commensurate with the persons' psychological capacities" (APA, 1992, standard 4.02c) and seek assent to the interventions. Consent should be obtained from a legally authorized person, as permitted by law.

In many professional association's codes, such as the American Counseling Association's Code of Ethics and Standards of Practice, practitioners are encouraged to make full disclosures to patients, both at the initiation of the work and during the work. This is a very realistic standard for the psychotherapy process since the issues of time and duration play a significant role. Pope and Vasquez (1991) state "As the treatment plan undergoes significant evolution, the patient must adequately understand these changes and voluntarily agree to them" (p.75).

What type of therapeutic information is disclosed with the intent of informed consent? "Counselors inform clients of the purposes, goals, techniques, procedures, limitations, potential risks, and benefits of services to be performed, and other pertinent information. Counselors take steps to ensure that clients understand the implications of diagnosis, the intended use of tests and reports, fees, and billing arrangements" (National Board of Certified Counselors, 1997, Section B8). Additionally, O'Neill (1998) believes that specific information about alternative treatments should be included even if they are out of the therapist's scope of training and experience, thus necessitating a referral.

INSURANCE ISSUES

In instances when patients have insurance coverage for psychotherapy, the fee is agreed to in advance (as with other patients) and charges must be billed appropriately and ethically. An important ethical principle here involves non-exploitation and integrity. The decision as to who receives the billing is made by the therapist and patient (unless a managed care company is involved and has specific requirements): it would be acceptable to bill either the patient or insurance company directly.

Billing should clearly reflect the specific services provided, the disorders being treated, as well as the co-payment received. For example, telephone sessions need to be indicated as such, not listed as an individual psychotherapy session within the office. Insurance bills should indicate customary fees. An unethical practice is to create a bill reflecting a higher fee than regularly charged for that specific service. Whenever fees are adjusted, the bill reflects this activity, even when the result is a lower payment from the insurance provider.

Good-faith attempts to collect the patient's co-payment portion of fees are required. When acting in good faith, in some instances, the psychotherapist may eventually be faced with writing off the patient's unpaid portion of fees at the conclusion of therapy. With a cancellation or unexpected missed appointment, the insurance company may not be billed, since services were not delivered. This issue is preferably addressed with the patient during the initial stage of psychotherapy as part of gaining informed consent. Often the therapist informs the patient of the expectations and responsibilities regarding cancellations. It is considered ethically responsive to reduce the total fees when a patient experiences a financial crisis. A mutually agreed upon fee affordable for the patient is in the best interest of the patient.

INVOLUNTARY HOSPITALIZATION

In California, when a patient is believed to be a danger to others, or to himself or herself, or gravely disabled due to a mental disorder, the county may, upon probable cause, provide for an involuntary 72 hour hold for treatment and evaluation at an approved psychiatric health facility. This procedure may be invoked by a county designated person such as a member of a crisis team, a sheriff, a police officer, or a mental health professional. This procedure is authorized by California Welfare and Institutions Code Section 5150.

A psychotherapist may become involved in initiating an involuntary hospitalization when the therapist has reasonable cause to believe that a patient meets any of the above stated criteria. Contacting the appropriate county designated professional, such as the Psychiatric Emergency Team, or Psychiatric Assessment Team, and explaining the situation, is an acceptable breach of patient-psychotherapist confidentiality.

Under the social policy of "deinstitutionalization", involuntary hospitalization, also known as confinement or commitment, is sought after less restrictive measures or alternatives have failed. The legal doctrine of using the least restrictive alternative requires that treatment be no more harsh, hazardous, or intrusive than necessary to achieve the therapeutic aims and to protect patients and others from physical harm.

Sound clinical practice includes a first attempt to arrange for the patient to voluntarily hospitalize him or herself for appropriate psychiatric assessment and treatment, before seeking involuntary hospitalization. Note:Only specifically county designated individuals may authorize an involuntary confinement. As mentioned above, treating psychotherapists may initiate involuntary confinements by requesting the services of a mobile Psychiatric Assessment Team or Psychiatric Emergency Team or other county designated professionals.

MARRIAGE & DISSOLUTION LAWS

Laws regarding marriage and dissolution of marriage may provide valuable information for the practicing psychotherapist. For example, California is one of the states where common law marriage does not exist. Unfortunately, many unmarried couples mistakenly believe that if they reside in the same household for a minimum number of years (often 7) they have all the legal rights of a married couple. Additionally, minors experience an increase of rights once legally married, being treated as adults by psychotherapists. Legally, marriage is a civil contract between a man and woman who have each provided consent, "followed by the issuance of a marriage license and solemnization" (Family Code Section 300). This information is provided to round out some knowledge, however, if a patient requests legal information, a referral to an attorney for legal advice is essential.

Marriage: Minors wishing to marry are required to obtain written consent of a parent or legal guardian as well as a court order granting permission (as per Family Code Section 302a & 302b). However, premarital counseling is required (Family Code Section 304).

Termination of Marriage: Dissolution of marriage replaced divorce as the legal term in the 1970's. Either spouse may initiate the dissolution on a no-fault basis, and the primary operable legal ground is a claim of irreconcilable differences.

The other ground for dissolution of marriage is incurable insanity (Family Code Section 2312). The dissolution may be finalized as early as six months after the service of summons and petition.

Property Settlement: Community property assets (all property acquired during marriage, aside from gifts, inheritance, and separate proceeds of previously owned money or property), and community debts are divided equally, unless spouses agree otherwise.

Child Custody: The courts have jurisdiction to modify custody, visitation, and related legal rights of the parents at any time until the child is 18 years old. The guiding principle is that custody is determined in accordance with the best interests of the child. In order to determine this, a child custody evaluation may be ordered by the court (Superior Court, e.g., 730 Evaluation in California) or a required formal mediation process would be enlisted. Although the order of custody preference spelled out in Family Code Section 3040 begins with joint custody, in high conflict or violent parental relationships, joint custody is not recommended, since the continued violence, argumentativeness, and bitterness between the parents has been shown to be detrimental to the children. Johnston and Campbell (1993) reported five types of interpersonal violence seen within custody disputes and the impact on the children. For more information, see section under Child Custody Evaluation.

Child Support: The decision concerning the amount paid by the parent(s) is based upon the need of the child, ability of the parent(s) to pay, and percentage of time spent with the child. A standardized computer program, Dissomaster, is currently employed in California. Rather than be at the discretion of the court, the computer program creates the support figures based on the mother's and father's income, child care costs, other expenses, and the amount of time spent with the child. Either or both parents may be ordered to pay what is necessary for the support, maintenance, and education of the child. The amount is always subject to later modification until the child is 18 years old.

Spousal Support: The amount awarded to a spouse (formerly called alimony) is based upon need and ability to pay. Consideration is often given to the duration of the marriage and the employability of the spouse seeking support. The amount and terms may be modified by the Court at any time. Support is terminated upon death of their spouse, remarriage of the spouse receiving support, or other contingencies provided for in the settlement agreement or order.

MEDIATION

Mediation is a confidential process to assist divorcing or divorced parents work out an agreement about custody and visitation issues. A neutral setting is provided and the parents meet together and develop an agreement that is in the best interests of the child or children. A skilled and trained individual (often with a minimum of a Masters of Arts degree plus training and experience in conflict resolution) works as a mediator to assist the parents in this resolution process. The aim is to work out a parenting plan and set aside fault and blame. Many jurisdictions have mediation services connected to the Superior Court. California law requires that couples who disagree with the child custody or visitation orders must attend mediation before their court hearing on the matter.

When domestic violence is an issue, or a restraining order (protective order) is in effect, mediation can begin with separate interviews of the parents, and the parents can be escorted to and from their cars, or in and out of the court building by marshals. A parenting plan is created in these instances, in which the child's and victim's safety is assured. For further exploration of mediation standards, The Academy of Family

Mediators has developed Standards of Practice (Academy of Family Mediators, 1988).

MINORS - TREATMENT OF

The following section presents ethical and legal aspects involved in the treatment of minors. Two important legal aspects are listed below:

- No minor under 12 can receive outpatient mental health counseling without parental consent.
- All minors who are emancipated can receive outpatient counseling without parental consent.

CONFIDENTIALITY - Minors

Generally, minors (under age 18) are entitled to the protection of confidentiality unless there is an applicable legal or ethical exception. Exceptions are the same as with adult patients (e.g. threats of violence to another, or suicide; reporting abuse; patient gravely disabled; etc.). An additional exception is the right of parents to inspect the therapist's records concerning their child when the treatment is with parental consent. If full disclosure is not in the best interests of the minor patient, therapist can provide a summary, and use arbitration if necessary to determine minimum disclosure. If unsatisfactory, wait for court order to disclose more.

Privilege of Confidentiality

With respect to a situation in which a minor has requested and been given mental health treatment pursuant to an exception, the minor holds the privilege. This also applies if she or he is treated as an adult due to emancipation. (Evidence Code § 1014.5 has been eliminated and is no longer specified in law

- this referred to the psychotherapist holding the privilege). The patient has the right to assert Privilege as a means of blocking disclosure of confidential information during a court or other legal proceeding. The holder of the privilege has this right. If the minor has a court appointed legal guardian or conservator that individual becomes the holder of the privilege.

When Parental Consent is Required for Treatment
Consent must always be secured for treatment of individuals under 12 years of age.

Treatment of Minors Without Parental Consent: Legally permissible when the minor consents and is either legally emancipated, or meets the criteria on an exception within specific preconditions and treatable clinical issues. However, when treating under an exception, parental consent must be obtained at any later time that is deemed appropriate.

Specific Preconditions and Treatable Clinical Issues Exception:

1. Preconditions Required:
   a) 12 or older;
   b) Sufficiently mature to participate intelligently;
   c) Therapy is on an outpatient basis; and
   d) Good reason for treating without parental consent.

2. Treatable Clinical Issues:
   a) Minor would present a danger of serious physical or mental harm to him or herself or to others without treatment. Family Code § 6924;
   b) Minor has been the alleged victim of incest or child abuse (including rape);
   c) Another treatable issue is when the minor seeks therapy for diagnosis or treatment of drug or alcohol related problems and the therapist is a

provider under contract with the state or a county to provide alcohol or drug abuse counseling services. Family Code § 6929;

d) Minor may consent to medical care related to the prevention or treatment of pregnancy, except sterilization or abortion. Family Code § 6925.

Record Keeping: When treating without parental consent, the therapist must state in the minor's records whether or when attempts were made to contact parents or legal guardian and whether such attempts were successful or reasons why such contact would be inappropriate.

Applicable Laws Regarding the Treatment of Minors

Family Code § 6924:
A minor who is 12 years or older may consent to mental health treatment or counseling on an outpatient basis if both of the following requirements are satisfied:

(1) The minor, in the opinion of the attending professional person, is mature enough to participate intelligently in the outpatient services.

(2) The minor would present a danger of serious physical or mental harm to self or to others without the mental health treatment or counseling or is the alleged victims of incest or child abuse.

Family Code § 6929:
A minor who is 12 years of age or older may consent to medical care and counseling relating to the diagnosis and treatment of a drug or alcohol related problem. As used in this section, "counseling" means the provision of counseling services by a provider under contract with the state or a county to provide alcohol or drug abuse counseling services. The consent of parent, parents or legal guardian shall not be necessary to authorize these services. Mental health treatment or coun-

seling shall include the involvement of minor's parent, parents or legal guardian, unless in the opinion of the professional person who is treating the minor, such involvement would be inappropriate. The therapist shall state in the patient record whether and when (date and time) he or she attempted to contact the parent, parents or legal guardian of the minor, and whether such attempt was successful or unsuccessful, or the reason why, in his or her opinion, it would be inappropriate to contact the parent, parents or legal guardian of the minor.

An often misunderstood point regarding a minor's psychotherapy records concerns the non-custodial parent. A non-custodial parent has a right to access his or her child's records. Access to records and information pertaining to a minor child, cannot be denied because the parent is not the child's custodial parent. However, under certain circumstances addressed in the Health and Safety Code Section 1795.14, a therapist may withhold the records: "The representative of a minor shall not be entitled to inspect or obtain copies of the minor's patient records under . . . the following circumstances . . . Where the health care provider determines that access to the patient records would have a detrimental effect on the provider's professional relationship with the minor patient or the minor's physical safety or psychological well-being" (Health and Safety code § 1795.14).

Emancipated Minors.

Any person under the age of 18 years who comes within the following description is an emancipated minor:

(a) Who has entered into a valid marriage, whether or not such marriage was terminated by dissolution; or
(b) Who is on active duty with any of the Armed Forces of the United States of America (minors 16 and older may enlist); or
(c) Who has received a declaration of emancipation from the superior court of the county. A minor

must be at least 14 years old before he or she can receive such a declaration.

Treatment of Minors without Parental Consent

- Emancipated Minor, or
- 12 or older
- Sufficiently Mature
- Outpatient Therapy
- Good Reason for Treating

MULTIPLE RELATIONSHIPS

Multiple relationships with patients occur when a psychotherapist "engages in another, significantly different relationship with the patient" (Pope, 1991, p. 21). Ethical problems often emerge when therapists expand their professional relationship with a patient into another kind of relationship. Of course, multiple relationships may be inevitable where it is not feasible to avoid social and nonprofessional contact, such as in small communities (Biaggio & Greene, 1995). Small communities may be designated by geography such as rural communities (Gates & Speare, 1990), or affiliation, as in ethnic minority communities (Sears, 1990) and gay or lesbian communities (Smith, 1990). In fact, Berman (1990) developed the term *overlapping relationships* to describe the unavoidable types of multiple relationships that may occur for therapists and their patients. The American Psychological Association also acknowledged "In many communities and situations, it may not be feasible or reasonable for psychologists to avoid social or other nonprofessional contacts with persons such as patients, clients, students, supervisees, or research participants" (1992, p. 1601).

These overlapping types of relationships are considered to be problematic if they impair the therapist's objectivity or harm or exploit the patient. Fortunately, the Feminist Therapy Code of Ethics (Feminist Therapy Institute, 1987) provides guidelines regarding the management of overlapping relationships. The guidelines encourage the self-monitoring of one's public and private statements and strictly prohibits any sexual intimacies or overtly or covertly sexualized behaviors with a client or former client (Section IIIa,b,c). Directly addressing the possibilities of running into patients within small communities provides information on how to handle these situations in the patient's best interest. In most ethical codes, the therapist is responsible for maintaining professional boundaries, thus a therapist initiated discussion would provide an opportunity for the patient to disclose thoughts and feelings about these potential encounters prior to their occurrence.

From a slightly different perspective, Arons and Siegel (1995) described the consequences of finding oneself in unexpected situations with patients, such as encountering a patient while engaging in religious or political activities, or at a nude beach, or in a queue for an x-rated film. They paralleled the therapist's experience to the exposure of the Wizard of Oz by Toto; being seen in one's full human vulnerability by a patient, the way the wizard was seen once the cloth curtain was pulled aside. They noted feelings of shame and inadequacy and concerns about losing patients. These feelings and concerns can affect the therapeutic relationship through the transference and countertransference. Preparing for these kinds of encounters through imaginal exercises or personal psychotherapy can provide "insight into which parts of our professional persona are there to support our work and which parts stem from our fears, self-criticism, and difficulty accepting unexamined aspects of ourselves" (p. 134). Self-exploration around these issues can benefit the psychotherapist as well as the patient.

Multiple relationship violations can result in license suspension or revocation actions and potential civil liability if sued by a patient. They are primarily an ethical rather than a legal prohibition, with the exception of sexual relationships, which are legal prohibitions (see Psychotherapist-Patient Sexual Intimacy section). Psychotherapists must be cognizant of their potentially influential position with respect to patients, and they avoid exploiting the trust and dependency of such persons, avoiding multiple relationships with patients that could impair their professional judgment or increase the risk of exploitation.

Multiple Relationships Generally Include:

1. Sexual relationships.
2. Bartering or trading for services. Although not prohibited, psychotherapists ordinarily refrain from bartering because such arrangements create inherent risks, potential for conflicts, exploitation, and distortion of the professional relationship. One may barter only if it is not clinically contraindicated, and the relationship is not exploitative.
3. Business or financial transactions outside the scope of the professional therapy relationship.
4. Supervisorial or teacher-student relationships.
5. Social relationships that interfere with the best interests of the patient.

Psychotherapists Avoid:

- exploiting the trust of patients
- multiple relationships with patients that could impair their professional judgment or increase the risk of exploitation

PRIVILEGED COMMUNICATIONS

Psychotherapist-patient communications are considered privileged communications. Patients can freely express themselves, describing the problems and issues they are facing in an honest and open manner. The privilege can benefit and protect the patient, however it does not offer protection in all instances. Limitations on the scope of the privilege are covered later in this section. A communication considered privileged is a "communication that the holder of the privilege must authorize disclosure of and testimony about" (Caudill & Pope, 1995, p. 171). The psychotherapist-patient privilege is codified by statute, which means it is defined by law.

Privilege of Confidentiality Rule

The focus here is within the context of legal proceedings where attempts are made to have the content of confidential patient therapist communications revealed. No disclosure can properly be made by the therapist to anyone else unless there is an appropriate waiver of the privilege or the privilege is limited by an exception.

Who May Assert to Waive the Privilege:

Privilege may only be asserted or waived by the holder of the privilege. This is usually the patient, but under Evidence Code 1015 the psychotherapist is required to assert the privilege, to "claim" the privilege on the patient's behalf, when a party attempts to have a psychotherapist reveal the content of a patient's communication in a legal proceeding. Without an appropriate waiver, the sought after information remains confidential, and is not subject to disclosure.

Waiver of Privilege

Patient may waive the privilege. There is no privilege if it has been waived by the patient (the holder of the privilege).

If a patient wishes to have the patient-therapist communications disclosed in a legal proceeding, the therapist cannot prevent him or her from doing so.

• It is essential to remember that the patient, even if a minor, is generally the holder of the privilege. The Evidence Code names only three holders of the privilege:

1. The patient;
2. Legal guardian or conservator of the patient;
3. Personal representative of the patient if the patient is deceased.

Limitations to Privilege

The following limitations to privilege illustrate the range of situations that require or permit the disclosure of confidential communications. These are most common to the psychotherapist-patient relationship. All are set forth in the California Evidence Code. (Readers interested in other exceptions are referred to Evidence Code Section 1017, court appointed evaluator; Section 1019, parties claiming through deceased patient; Section 1021, intention of deceased patient concerning writing affecting property interest; Section 1022, validity of writing affecting property interest; Section 1026, required report to public employee):

1. Patient under 16, victim of crime.

There is no privilege if the patient is a child under 16, and the psychotherapist has reasonable cause to believe that the patient has been the victim of a crime and that disclosure of the communication is in the best interest of the child (Evidence Code § 1027).

2. Dangerous patient exception.

There is no privilege under Evidence Code Section 1024. Patient is dangerous to himself or others or property of others and therapist has reasonable cause to believe this is the case, and the disclosure is necessary to prevent the threatened danger. This law is broader than the other exceptions to privilege, in that, besides applying to legal proceedings, it also applies to the clinical setting.

3. Crime or tort.

There is no privilege if the patient sought therapy to aid in planning, committing, escaping punishment, detection, or apprehension regarding a crime or tort (Evidence Code § 1018).

4. Patient-Litigant exception.

There is no privilege when the patient's emotional condition is raised as an issue by patient or his/her representative, examples include a worker's compensation suit regarding stress, a proceeding to determine sanity in a criminal action suit, or proceedings to establish competence (Evidence Code § 1016).

5. Breach of Duty Arising Out of Psychotherapist-Patient Relationship.

There is no privilege when either a psychotherapist or patient alleges a breach of duty arising out of the psychotherapist-patient relationship (e.g., within a malpractice lawsuit). This law has limited applicability outside the context of legal proceedings, e.g., if a patient refuses to pay his or her bill for therapy, the therapist may reveal information relevant to collecting payment (i.e., the patient's name and address and the amount owed), but no other information, to a collection agencies should notify patients of this practice at the outset of therapy (Evidence Code § 1020).

6. Proceeding to Establish Competence.

There is no privilege in a proceeding brought by or on behalf of the patient to establish his competence (Evidence Code § 1025). Competence hearings focus on capacities to understand, to act reasonably, to carry out duties.

7. Proceeding to Determine Sanity.

There is no privilege in a proceeding to determine a

patient's sanity (Evidence Code § 1023). Insanity is a complex legal term signifying lack of criminal responsibility to some degree.

8. Court or Legally Mandated Disclosure.

Examples, Reporting child, dependent adult, or elder abuse (see Welfare and Institutions Code § 15632a); These are restricted disclosures. Fortunately, child abuse, dependent adult abuse, and elder abuse reports are themselves confidential (Penal Code § 11166; Welfare and Institutions Code § 15630-15631).

Holder of the Privilege

1. The patient;
2. Legal guardian or conservator of the patient;
3. Personal representative of the patient if the patient is deceased.

PSYCHOTHERAPIST-PATIENT SEXUAL INTIMACY

Criminally Prohibited Acts: Any kind of sexual contact, asking for sexual exploitation, or sexual misconduct by a psychotherapist with a patient is categorized as illegal, unethical, and unprofessional. *Sexual contact* means touching an intimate part (sexual organ, anus, buttocks, groin, or breast) of another person. *Touching* means physical contact with another person either through the person's clothes or directly with the person's skin (e.g. intercourse, fondling, etc.). *Sexual misconduct* includes nudity, kissing, spanking, as well as sexual suggestions or innuendoes. The above prohibitions are applicable both during the professional relationship, and for two years following termination of therapy. Penalties: The first offense is a misdemeanor. Subsequent violations are treated either as misdemeanor or felony violations. Any proven offense also subjects the therapist to license suspension and/or revocation, and civil liability.

When Patient(s) Report Sexual Misconduct of Prior Therapist(s): Any psychotherapist who becomes aware that his or her patient had alleged sexual intercourse or sexual contact with a previous psychotherapist during the course of a prior treatment, shall provide the patient a brochure promulgated by the Department of Consumer Affairs which delineates the rights of and remedies for patients who have been sexually involved with their psychotherapist. Furthermore, the psychotherapist is required to discuss the contents with the patient. No breach of confidentiality is permitted in these instances.

RECORD KEEPING GUIDELINES

Acting in a professional manner requires keeping some basic patient records and notes concerning patients' biographical, residential, employment, and related basic information; as well as legally required entries such as indicating the reason a minor was treated without parental consent and the efforts made to contact the parents if appropriate. Knowing the documentation requirements of the institution in which one works is also essential. Additional reasons for records and notes include:

a) Treatment continuity provided by the therapist;
b) Helping transition to other therapists, or when patient returns to therapy after a substantial time gap;
c) Verification of mental status for disability, insurance company requirements, and workers' compensation claims;
d) A resource for future research, writing, or teaching;
e) Liability protection if therapist is called upon to justify

treatment (whether in a court case, lawsuit, or ethics committee investigation). In fact when a psychologist knows the records will be subject to legal scrutiny, he or she is ethically bound to create records in the quality and detail that would be useful in the proceedings (APA, 1992, standard 1.23b).

However, under some circumstances it may be in the best interests of the patient to limit the content of the notes and records. Keep in mind that whatever data or information is placed in patient notes and records is subject to potential full disclosure in some form of legal proceeding.

Content and Length of Records and Notes

No clear legal or ethical standards of practice speak to the overall content and length of patient records and notes. For the most part, these are discretionary decisions for the psychotherapist. Some practitioners favor lengthy and detailed notes; while others prefer brief and sketchy ones. The basic rule is acting in the best interest of the patient, and clearly reasonable minds may differ on what this requires. Content of records minimally include: "identifying data, dates of services, types of services, fees, any assessment, plan for intervention, consultation, summary reports, release of information documents, and testing reports" (APA, 1993, 1B).

Access to Records and Notes

These confidential documents belong to the therapist, and should be kept in a locked, safe, and secure place. The therapist is responsible for the safety and confidentiality of the record. The patient has the right to request copies, and the therapist, for good reason can provide only a summary. If a patient insists on full access, and the therapist objects, mediation is the next level of response. Ultimately, if records and notes are subpoenaed, it is prudent to refuse access until ordered by a court to comply.

REFERRALS AND ADJUNCTIVE SERVICES

In the practice of psychotherapy and in your role as therapist, you are involved in a variety of ongoing assessments, including initially striving to identify the patient's needs and then to recognize and acknowledge your own limitations with regard to those needs. Appropriate referrals are made with the patient's best interest in mind.

Two major categories of referrals are presented below, essential and complementary. Additionally, a myriad of commonly used referrals are included to assist you in discerning the specific referral sources needed for your particular case. Hopefully, these will: provide you with resources to strengthen your case management ability; assist you in developing case presentations; enhance your ability to respond to vignettes in a comprehensive manner for an oral examination; and provide resources for your future work with patients.

I. Essential Referrals

These occur in emergencies or crises, such as when medical attention is called for, and in situations where all trained psychotherapists would likely utilize an adjunctive service.

Several examples follow:

A potential patient presents the psychotherapist with a conflict of interest; the usual ethical course of action is to refer to another therapist.

A patient presenting with a possible neurological dysfunction; a medical screening and neuro-psychological evaluation would be essential prior to engagement in psychotherapy.

A chemically dependent individual or family presenting with these issues should be referred to available adjunctive services such as 12-step programs (Alcoholics Anonymous, Al-Anon, Al-Ateen, etc.).

II. Complementary Referrals

This category of referral goes beyond the emergency or crisis situation and is meant to provide an enrichment to the psychotherapeutic process. An example is referring a couple you are working with to a couples communication training group or referring parents to a parenting class such as Systematic Training for Effective parenting or Parent Effectiveness Training.

Commonly Utilized Referrals and Adjuncts

This is an example of some resources that may exist within your community.

Crisis Referrals

- Emergency Room: Immediate medical or psychiatric assistance. Alternatively, some communities have mobile Psychiatric Assessment Teams.
- Law Enforcement Agency such as Police or Sheriff's Department: useful when following through with the Tarasoff warning; Ch ild Abuse Report; Protection of the patient or therapist
- Hotline: Information, Referral and Support for patient or family members
- Rape Crisis Center: Crisis counseling, Ongoing Counseling, support, family and partner assistance
- Shelter: Safe respite; Shelter for homeless or battered women and children
- Social Services: Child and adult protective services; assistance with money, food, clothing, and shelter. General relief is a service generally designed for the homeless.

Clinically Related Adjunctive Referrals

- Child Psychologist or Child Psychotherapist: Special expertise in working with children
- Clinical Psychologist: Psychological testing
- College or University Counseling Centers: Helpful for patients who are students, often provide low-cost services, such as short-term topical groups
- Group Therapy: Adjunctive or sole treatment
- Neuropsychologist: Neuropsychological evaluation
- Pastoral Counselor or Clergy: Religious or spiritual
- Psychiatrist: Psychopharmacological consultation
- Residential Treatment: Structured and specialized.
- School Guidance Counselor: Guidance in vocational opportunities, future academic development
- Sex Therapist: Sexual dysfunction that you are not qualified to treat
- Vocational Counselor: Occupational testing; Career development and counseling

Legal Resources

- American Civil Liberties Union
- Attorney or Legal Clinic or Legal Assistance Center
- Attorney General's Office
- District Attorney's Office: Generally provide victims and witnesses of crimes with information and resources; information on court hearings.
- Family Violence Legal Center or Battered Woman's Legal Office: information on obtaining restraining orders
- Licensing Boards or Professional Associations: To register ethical complaints with board or association
- Patients' Rights Advocate: Assists psychiatric patients with information, violation or denial of rights, representation at civil certification review hearings

Educational or Occupational Resources

- School Systems: Pupil personnel service and attendance counselors; nurses; Special education services;

Services for students with disabilities
- Library: Resources for information and research
- Child's School: Principal or teacher for school related child and/or family problems
- Employment Development Department: Employment services
- Social Services: Welfare services, employment assistance, In-home care
- Employment agencies: Job recruitment, placement, and training
- Employee Assistance Program: Employee services for issues interfering with job satisfaction or productivity.

Medically Related Referrals
- Family Physician: Physical exams to rule out organic causes; consult with eating disorder team
- Neurologist: To assess and diagnosis organic mental disorders
- Veterans Administration (VA) Hospital
- Psychiatrist: Consultation and Medication Evaluation
- Urologist or Gynecologist
- HIV Testing Center; AIDS Projects
- Hospice Care; Skilled Nursing Facility
- Physical Therapy; Bodywork; Massage
- Detoxification Center
- Registered Dietitian

Self-Help and Support Groups
- Coming Out Groups; Gay Men's Groups; Lesbian Groups
- Alcoholics Anonymous (*currently over 150 Anonymous groups*)
- Al Anon; Alateen, Alatot
- CoDA Group: CoDependents Anonymous
- Cocaine or Narcotics Anonymous
- Sex Addicts Anonymous
- Dreamtending or Dream Work Groups
- Adult Children of Alcoholics: ACA groups, ACOA

workshops
- Eating Disorder Groups: Overeaters Anonymous; Specifically focused group therapy.
- Survivor Groups such as Incest Survivors: Daughters United, Daughters and Sons United; Incest Survivors Anonymous; Men's survivor groups.
- Survivor Groups (other Traumas): Children of Holocaust Survivors; Plane Crash Survivors; Prisoners of War
- Parents Groups: Parent Effectiveness Training (PET); Systematic Training for Effective Parenting (STEP); Parents United
- Support Groups for Patient's Families
- Smoking Cessation Groups
- Specific Racial or Ethnic or Cultural Support Group
- Singles Groups: Parents Without Partners for single parents; community organizations such as YMCA, YWCA, churches

Referral Process

In contemplating and making referrals, the therapist needs to consider a number of factors, including:

1. Familiarity with the referral source, including the services offered, ethical treatment provided, and quality of services.

2. Which specific person, community agency, or service is best qualified to help the patient.

3. Limitations or constraints that would make it difficult for the patient to gain or benefit, e.g., geographic or physical inaccessibility, unaffordable cost, or language.

4. Whether the therapist should reach out or whether the patient should make the contact with the referral source; or whether a meeting with the referral source, the therapist, and the patient should occur.

5. The patient's readiness and willingness to access the referral.

6. Legal and ethical issues that emerge with a referral - confidentiality being the primary one.

REFERRING CASE OUT

It is considered ethical practice to disengage and refer the patient out for therapy when it would be improper for you to be, or continue to be, the psychotherapist in the case. Several situations follow:

- The case is outside your scope of practice or the course of therapy is outside your level of training and experience. Examples of cases outside scope of practice could include a referral for conducting a battery of neuropsychological tests. A referral for conducting a child custody evaluation could be outside your scope of training.

- You have had previous relationships with the potential patient, such as a friendship, or the potential patient is related to you, or is your student.

- Potential patient is in a family, friendship, or intimate relationship with an existing patient causing unresolvable boundary or confidentiality issues.

- You become aware of how countertransference is interfering with your ability to provide effective psychotherapy, and you are unable to address it sufficiently through a range of methods including personal therapy, consultation, or supervision. The best interest of your patient is clearly an active principle here.

- Having obtained peer or other professional consultation, and concluding you are not effectively treating the patient, and are unable to do so, you must refer the patient to a more capable psychotherapist. If the patient is not appreciably benefitting from treatment, a referral is in his or her best interest.

RELEASE OF INFORMATION

It is essential to obtain an appropriate release (preferably written) before breaching therapist-patient confidentiality. This written release includes the patient's written consent.

Guidelines for release of information:

- Absent an applicable legal* or ethical exception, everything disclosed by a patient to a therapist is considered confidential, including the therapist's thoughts based on such information (e.g., diagnosis), and is not to be disclosed to anyone else. This includes the fact that the patient is in therapy. *Legal exception: A provider of health care may speak with another licensed person regarding the patient, if purpose is for diagnosis or treatment of the patient (Civil Code § 56).

- A release from confidentiality is one of the exceptions which allows the therapist to divulge otherwise confidential information. The release must be secured from the patient, and it is good practice (although not mandatory) to secure the release from confidentiality in writing.

- Releases are commonly secured from the patient in conjunction with referrals to other helping professionals such as physicians, psychiatrists, or other therapists. They are also routinely obtained when the patient is referred in by someone else such as a probation officer, school counselor, or minister.

- Releases are also commonly utilized by insurance or managed care companies as a prerequisite to payment, so that a representative of the company may speak with the therapist about the treatment issues and related therapeutic actions.

- Even if the patient has given his or her other therapist, physician, or minister permission to talk with you, you still need a release from the patient before you can breach your confidential relationship with the patient, absent another applicable exception.

SCOPE OF PRACTICE

All psychotherapists are required to practice within a specifically defined scope, pursuant to the licensing law of the profession. Marriage and family therapists are licensed by the California Board of Behavioral Sciences pursuant to the Business and Professions Code § 4980. Psychologists are licensed by the Board of Psychology pursuant to the Business and Professions Code § 2903.

- Within the Scope of Practice
  Marriage and Family Therapist

  Marriage and family therapists may practice psychotherapy and diagnose and treat mental disorders as long as the focus is on some aspect of resolving interpersonal issues, such as achieving more satisfying and productive relationships. This includes working with groups, families, couples, dyads of any configuration, and individuals.

According to the Business and Professions Code § 4980.02: "The applications of marriage, family, and child counseling principles and methods includes, but is not limited to, the use of applied psychotherapeutic techniques, to enable individuals to mature and grow within marriage and the family, and the provision of explanations and interpretations of the psychosexual and psychosocial aspects of relationships."

Psychological testing may be used within the course of a marriage and family therapists' practice. Based on the California Attorney General's opinion (1984) on psychological testing, marriage and family therapists have the statutory authority to use psychological tests "within the course of their practice, within their field or fields of competence as established by education, training, and experience, and where such tests could and would be used to examine an interpersonal relationship between spouses or member of a family to help achieve a more adequate, satisfying and productive marriage and family adjustment."

- Outside Scope of Practice
  Marriage and Family Therapist:

  When focus of therapy would not be on some aspect of resolving relationship or interpersonal issues. Treating someone for smoking cessation, accepting referrals for conducting neuropsychological assessments, or doing a worker's compensation evaluation can be deemed to be outside the scope of practice for a Marriage and Family Therapist.

Practical Reality:

Many issues impact the quality of interpersonal interactions with another, and may be within the scope of practice. Who is in the room for psychotherapy is not the relevant question as Marriage and Family Therapists regularly work with individual patients within the scope of their practice.

- Within Scope of Practice
  Psychologist:

  The practice of psychology is defined broader than the practice of marriage and family therapy. The Business and Professions Code § 2903 states: "The practice of psychology is defined as rendering or offering to render for a fee to individuals, groups, organizations or the public any psychological service involving the application of psychological principles, methods, and procedures of understanding, prediction, and influencing behavior, such as the principles pertaining to learning, perception, motivation, emotions, and interpersonal relationships: and the methods and procedures of interviewing, counseling, psychotherapy, behavior modification, and hypnosis; and of constructing, administering, and interpreting tests of mental abilities, aptitudes, interests, attitudes, personality characteristics, emotions, and motivations."

- Outside Scope of Practice
  Psychologist:

  An example of working outside the scope of practice would be the prescription of medication. This is currently not permitted, but legislative bills have been introduced with a movement in this direction. The Board of Psychology in California has encouraged all psychologists to obtain extensive training in psychopharmacology.

SCOPE OF TRAINING AND/OR EXPERIENCE

Once it is determined that the issues being addressed are within the Scope of Practice, the next filter is determining whether or not the treating therapist has sufficient training and/

or experience to act within the best interests of the patient in treating such issues. If yes, then the treatment proceeds. If no, then the treating therapist needs to either secure the required training (through education, supervision, research, consultation, etc.) within a reasonable time period, or she or he needs to refer the case out for treatment of the issues involved. For example, a patient reports the symptoms of bulimia during the fourth session of treatment for relationship difficulties, and the treating therapist has a reasonable amount of training in eating disorders, but does not have a reasonable amount of experience in dealing with this specialized issue. Prudent behavior on the part of the therapist involves obtaining supervision or consultation. However, depending on the therapist's limitations, referring the case out to a more experienced psychotherapist may be necessary.

SECRETS - Guidelines in Dealing with Secrets

As a prudent practice issue, it is suggested that therapists establish reasonable and consistent policies concerning how to handle secrets disclosed to the therapist by a patient in conjoint therapy. Approaches range from never disclosing to always disclosing all content. Whatever your particular policy will be, it is recommended to share this at the outset of treatment as part of obtaining informed consent for treatment. The following are several types of policies and practices:

1. During the initial session, the therapist may describe the basic intention in conjoint treatment: to say and hear everything *in session*, and that the therapist maintains the right to disclose confidential information, if he or she feels it is in the best interest of the patients. Some psychotherapists explain that they assume the holder of a secret wants help in disclosing it, which they will provide. This type of policy may be clarified if one spouse attempts to share a secret.

2. When a secret is disclosed to the therapist privately, he or she reminds the holder of the secret of the policy, and works toward disclosure (by the holder of the secret) in conjoint session. Example: Information regarding an affair or sexual liaison.

   If a patient refuses to reveal the secret:
   a) The therapist assesses whether or not the patient is committed to improving the relationship.
   b) If the patient is committed to improving the relationship, a referral for individual therapy might be advisable, to work through resistance to disclosing. Under this arrangement, conjoint therapy would continue, with the secret held until the disclosure was made.
   c) If the patient is not invested in improving or staying in the relationship, the therapist may use the conjoint session to make this explicit. Moreover, the therapist may no longer feel effective as the conjoint therapist, and may refer out for further therapy without giving the specific reason (i.e., that patient won't reveal secret).

3. Unusual or unique circumstances may present complex dilemmas for the therapist without an explicit policy. A therapist may choose to hold a secret confidential and continue working with the couple, if in his or her sound clinical judgment, it is in the best interest of the patient. An important question when working with a couple, is "who is the patient?" Each individual, or the relationship, or all of the above? The answer to this question may prove helpful to you in developing a policy, if you have not considered these issues yet. Reading the literature, consulting with colleagues, and discussing standards of practice in the field will be helpful for you in creating your working policy.

SUBPOENA

A subpoena is an order of the court, which compels a witness to appear at a particular location, such as a courtroom, at a specified time, to provide testimony and/or records. The setting may be within a court hearing, administrative hearing, or a deposition. A psychotherapist may receive a *subpoena duces tecum*, which is a subpoena for documentary evidence consisting of records, notes, and billing information. These types of subpoenas cover notes in any form, including books, papers, audiotapes, videotapes, and computer generated information (Evidence Code § 250). When served with a subpoena, prudent action consists of claiming the privilege and contacting the patient and the patient's attorney regarding the best course of action (and document the course of action suggested). In highly complex situations, where the patient and attorney disagree on your release of confidential information or records, you should also consider seeking legal consultation, since failure to appear at the specified time and place could result in contempt proceedings.

SUICIDAL IDEATION

Responding to a patient's potential for suicide can be one of the most troubling and intimidating tasks faced by clinicians, requiring a careful assessment and response. As many know, suicide remains the ninth leading cause of death in the United States (Centers for Disease Control, 1997) and occurs more frequently than homicide. The clinical literature contains reports of the incidence and impact of patient suicidal behavior on interns and trainees (Kleespies, Penk, and Forsyth, 1993) as well as accomplished psychotherapists (Chemtob, Hamada, Bauer, Torigoe, & Kinney, 1988). The potential loss of a patient can evoke immense concerns for the patient and patient's family, in addition to serious concerns about the therapist's level of competence or continuation within the profession. Comprehensive clinical training in this area of suicide prevention and risk management will provide the practicing psychotherapist with adequate knowledge and experience to address these crises. Ongoing continuing education is encouraged for therapists to enhance their competent and ethical responsiveness.

A number of effective suicide prevention approaches have been proposed including action based approaches (Beck, Resnik, & Lettieri, 1986; Bongar, 1991), systematic methods to assess depression, suicide ideation, suicide plan, self-control, and suicide intent during intake interviews with suicidal patients (Sommers-Flanagan & Sommers-Flanagan, 1995), and integrated models combining affective and action-based interventions (Rosenberg, 1999). The following brief synopsis presents important elements in suicide prevention.

Assessment and Case Management of Suicidal Risk

Suicidality is measured primarily through a comprehensive clinical interview, review of ancillary information from previous outpatient and inpatient records, and psychological testing or use of assessment instruments such as questionnaires. Begin with a thorough clinical interview to assess suicidal risk. The risk can be measured on a continuum from mild, moderate, to severe. In managing suicidality, provide safety and structure, from management within the outpatient structure to involuntary hospitalization, when patient is imminently suicidal. Remember to consider the least restrictive interventions first.

Note: Although there is no legal requirement to report, there is ethical responsibility to intervene. The psychotherapist may need to break confidentiality by informing family, significant others, law enforcement professionals, or a psychiatric assessment and evaluation team. This is a situation in which confidentiality may be breached in order to prevent the patient from harming him or herself.

<u>Suicidal Potential: Assess</u>
Ideation
Intent
Level of Lethality

<u>Assess ideation, intent, and level of lethality</u>:

If there is ideation, assess the intent and the motivation to die, establish the precipitating factors, ask about the details of the plan, and the means considered. Inquire about the suicidal thoughts and feelings, and the frequency, intensity, and duration of these.

The intent of suicide is a risk factor to consider. "It can be helpful to have patients rate their suicidal intent on a scale of 1 to 10 (1 being no intent and 10 being total intent). Intent can be rated as absent, low, moderate, or high" (Sommers-Flanagan & Sommers-Flanagan, 1995, p. 45).

Plan - inquire about the specific details including the methods and the timeframe being considered.

Means - inquire what is being contemplated and how the means are available, e.g., weapon, rope, taking an overdose, jumping from bridge.

Risk Factors.

Higher rates of completed suicide are correlated with intent and more lethal methods, including firearms, strangulation, and overdose (Centers for Disease Control, 1997). These are considered significant risk factors. Even for children, suicide is correlated with an availability of firearms, e.g., guns figured in the suicides of 53% of children aged 1-14 years and 61% of children aged 15-18 (Zwillich, 1998).

A history of previously attempted suicide is a significant risk factor (Olin & Keatinge, 1998). Almost 80 percent of completed suicides were preceded by a prior attempt in a study by Schneidman (1975).

Other aspects to consider are the patient's sense of hopelessness, depressed mood, cognitive distortions, impaired thinking, impulsivity, intoxication, and judgment capacity. In regard to depressed mood, Resnik (1980) noted that suicide risk increases when the patient becomes anxious, agitated, or angry, indicating potential energy and increased motivation to carry out the suicide. Physical illness is also a contributing factor to risk, as is a history of psychiatric inpatient hospitalization (Olin & Keatinge, 1998; Pope & Vasquez, 1998).

Consider the presence of available deterrents. Significant deterrents involve the presence of support systems and the patient's willingness and capacity to seek these out, continued employment, financial resources, religious values, and spiritual beliefs.

SUICIDE RISK FACTORS

- Previous Attempt
- Substance Use
- Impulsivity
- Presence of Lethal Means
- Hopelessness
- Depressive Symptoms
- Psychopathology
- Financial Hardship
- Physical Illness
- Lack of social support

1. If Suicide is imminent:
   a) Work towards voluntary hospitalization,
   b) If patient refuses, initiate involuntary psychiatric hospitalization (Welfare and Institutions Code § 5150 - 72 hour psychiatric hold for evaluation and treatment) with police or other county designated personnel such as a Psychiatric Assessment Team, or Psychological Evaluation Mobile Team.
   c) Mobilize patient's support systems by notifying appropriate significant others.

2. If non-imminent - Suggested ways to manage suicidality:
   a) Note the protective or life enhancing aspects of the patient's self, such as the desire for help and a desire to live (Rosenberg, 1999).
   a) Work toward eliminating the means, such as giving a weapon to law enforcement for safekeeping.
   b) Intensify treatment by increasing frequency of sessions.
   c) Have patient notify his or her support network, or assist the patient in doing so. If necessary, a containment by the support system could be initiated, such as a 24 hour watch.
   d) Create a no-suicide contract with patient.
   e) Establish daily call-in policy.
   f) Give patient crisis or suicide hot line numbers and instructions on how to reach you in an emergency.
   g) Psychiatric or physician referral needs to be considered. For example, if patient is on medication, refer back to psychiatrist for medication re-evaluation and consult with this professional (Schutz, 1982).
   h) Address the emotional pain experienced by the patient, including the feelings of despair and hopelessness (Rosenberg, 1999), and the underlying thoughts and feelings of suicide (Schneidman, 1993). In doing so, ambivalence about dying and taking one's life may emerge, opening up more options for addressing the painful situation.

Document in your records: Document the results of the assessment, including ideation, intent, plan, means, previous attempts, your judgment about recurrent lethality; discussion with patient regarding the limits of confidentiality, other relevant information including family history, alcohol or drug use, severity of depression, other precipitating stressors, all actions taken, and results of actions.

Long Range Issues: Underlying difficulties such as substance abuse, depression, family history, chronic illness, and financial problems, will need to be focused upon for long range solution and problem solving.

SUICIDE - HIGH RISK

- Voluntary Hospitalization
- Involuntary Hospitalization
- Mobilize Patient's Support System

SUICIDE - LOW RISK

- Eliminate Means
- Intensify Treatment
- No-Suicide Contract
- Mobilize Support Network
- Physician Referral
- Daily Phone in Policy
- Emergency Phone Numbers
- Assess Emotional Pain

TARASOFF DECISION

When a patient communicates a serious threat of physical violence against a reasonably identifiable victim or victims, the therapist must operate as a *reasonably prudent practitioner* by making reasonable efforts to communicate the threat to the victim and to a law enforcement agency. "Psychotherapists who work with dangerous patients face a complex task of balancing the need of the patient for psychotherapy against the need of society for safety" (VandeCreek & Knapp, 1993, p.57). The therapist has an obligation to use reasonable care to protect the intended victim. This duty [to warn] is a required breach of confidentiality mandated by the *Tarasoff v. Regents of U.C.* court decision, and related legislation. Part of this duty may require warning individuals who could reasonably warn the intended victim. The preservation of life and safety is paramount within this decision. Related considerations include:

a) There is no *duty to warn* when the threat is made by someone other than the patient.

b) There is no *duty to warn* when there is no *reasonably identifiable* victim. For instance, when the patient describes a vague intention to go out and shoot unspecified people. However, if the patient threatened to go into a specific store and shoot people randomly, the persons in the store would probably be considered identifiable victims.

c) If the patient is believed to be a danger to others due to a mental disorder, then involuntary hospitalization may be appropriate (Welfare & Institutions Code § 5150).

d) The psychotherapist is exposed to criminal and civil liability, when he or she fails to provide an adequate warning of violence to the victim and law enforcement authorities.

Serious Threat of Physical Violence:

This is a phrase that is left open to interpretation, but it has been generally agreed that the term *serious* refers to the seriousness of the person's intentions rather than to the degree of violence threatened. Many have interpreted the term *serious* to mean *imminent*. One important note here: This decision does not require psychotherapists to reveal a patient's idle thoughts or expressed fantasies of harming others. The court was quite specific in referring to the importance of breaching confidentiality when such a disclosure would prevent the danger to the intended victim or victims.

Because of the considerable impact on the patient resulting from the act of revealing confidential information to another party, this type of information is essential to share as part of obtaining informed consent to treatment, and/or to review when a patient is making these serious threats. A small but intriguing empirical study by Beck (1982) indicated positive effects (or no effects) were associated with prior disclosure and discussion of the necessity to breach confidentiality. However, when there was no discussion, a negative effect was experienced.

TARASOFF DECISION

- Serious Threat of Physical Violence
- Duty to Warm Intended Victim (if Victim is Reasonably Identifiable) and,
- Law Enforcement Agency
- No Duty to Warn if Threat Made by someone other than patient

TERMINATION

Termination is an integral part of the therapeutic process. In addition to some of the ethical concerns outlined below, the termination process may provide the patient with opportunities for further growth, development, and change.

Timing of Termination Process

When feasible, a sufficient amount of time, or reasonable amount of time should be provided for termination and closure issues. The number of termination focused sessions is highly dependent on the length of the therapeutic relationship and the context of the treatment. If a therapist is working with patients on a time-limited basis, a referral to an appropriate provider would be given, but if the patient is in the midst of a crisis at the pre-specified end of therapy, then the therapist should address those needs until the crisis is resolved.

1. Therapeutic Response to Patient Concerns

The patient may present with direct or indirect expression of termination issues. For example, the patient may explicitly state that she or he is interested in terminating therapy (perhaps prematurely in your professional opinion), or it becomes clear that the patient has reached a point where it would be helpful to terminate (the original agreed upon goals have been reached and no other goals have been established). It may be helpful to assist the patient in acknowledging and validating his or her feelings, being aware of working towards an acceptable resolution.

2. Approaching Closure

Address any unfinished questions or business such as: Expression of thoughts or feelings that the patient and/or therapist could have done more, summarizing patient's perception of the therapy process, sharing positive and negative thoughts and feelings between patient and therapist, and evaluation of the positive aspects and possible disappointments concerning the therapeutic process.

3. Transitioning

Acknowledge patient's personal growth, summarize gains and successes, identify major "learnings" for both patient and therapist, discuss possible areas for future work and recommend future therapy alternatives if the patient is interested.

The responsibility to engage in a termination process belongs to the therapist. Note the following ethical principle:

"Prior to termination for whatever reason, except where precluded by the patient's or client's conduct, the psychologist discusses the patient's or client's views and needs, provides appropriate pre-termination counseling, suggests alternative service providers as appropriate, and takes other reasonable steps to facilitate transfer of responsibility to another provider if the patient or client needs one immediately" (APA, 1992, standard 4.09c).

TERMINATION

- Allow Sufficient Time for Termination Process
- Respond Therapeutically to Patient Concerns
- Acknowledge Patient's Growth
- Summarize Gains and Successes

TESTIMONY

Providing testimony within a court of law can be a stressful or frightening experience for psychotherapists unfamiliar with this process. Psychotherapists can be called as either fact witnesses or expert witnesses, however expert witnesses are directly hired as such in civil or criminal matters, to provide specialized knowledge to the trier of fact (judge). A fact witness is an individual subpoenaed to testify to the facts of a particular case. A psychotherapist may be called as a fact witness through a subpoena. Brodsky (1998) offered the following maxim "explicitly relax or engage in productive work just before your court appearance" (p. 112).

General Rule:

Without an applicable legal or ethical exception, therapists never testify regarding a patient because everything disclosed by a patient to a therapist is considered confidential, including the therapist's thoughts based on such information (such as the diagnosis and assessment). This includes the fact that the patient is in therapy. The following exceptions are most relevant in the context of testifying in court.

EXCEPTIONS

There are basic exceptions provided by law, where the therapist may breach confidentiality and disclose information provided by the patient:

1. Litigation exceptions:
   Patient's emotional condition is raised as an issue by patient or his or her legal representative;
   Litigation involving claimed breach of duty arising out of psychotherapist-patient relationship;
   Breach of duty suits by either patient or therapist: such as a malpractice claim or lawsuit against patient for nonpayment of previously agreed on fee.

2. Court appointed psychiatrist or psychologist: May testify if appointed at request of patient-defendant in criminal proceedings to determine whether or not to enter a plea of insanity.

3. Court or legally mandated disclosure: Some examples include reporting child, dependent adult, or elder abuse; or duty to warn about serious threat of bodily harm to a reasonably identifiable other (See privilege).

It is advisable to seek out consultation or legal counsel when confronted with a complex disclosable incident or situation.

UNPROFESSIONAL CONDUCT

Once licensed as a professional psychotherapist, one is held accountable for a range of behaviors related to the qualification, functions, or duties of a licensee. In California, the Board of Psychology and the Board of Behavioral Sciences may deny, suspend, or revoke the privilege to practice. Some gross departures from acceptable standards of practice are presented along with other circumstances that constitute unprofessional conduct.

- Unprofessional conduct includes performing or holding oneself out as able to perform professional services beyond one's field or field of competence as established by education, training, and/or experience (Business & Professions Code § 4982). Misrepresenting the type or status of a license is also included here.

- Failing to comply with the child abuse reporting requirements of Penal Code § 11166.

- Conviction of a crime substantially related to the qualifications, functions, or duties of a licensee.

- Using any controlled substance or specified dangerous drug, or any alcoholic beverage to a dangerous or injurious extent, or to the extent that such use impairs one's ability to conduct responsibilities with safety to the public. Also, conviction of more than one misdemeanor or any felony involving the use, consumption, or self-administration of any referred to substance.

- Intentionally or recklessly causing physical or emotional harm to any patient.

- Commission of any dishonest, or fraudulent act substantially related to the qualifications, functions, or duties of a licensee.

- Engaging in sexual relations with a patient, soliciting sexual relationship with a patient, or committing an act of sexual abuse, or sexual misconduct with a patient, or committing an act punishable as a sexually related crime, if substantially related to the qualifications, functions, or duties of a marriage, family, and child counselor.

- Failure to maintain confidentiality, except as otherwise required or permitted by law, of all information that has been received from a patient in confidence during the course of treatment and all information about the patient which is obtained from tests or other means.

- Regarding informed consent and practice: prior to the commencement of treatment, failing to disclose to the patient or prospective patient the fee to be charged for the professional services, or the basis upon which that fee will be computed.

- Paying, accepting, or soliciting any consideration, compensation, or remuneration, for the referral of professional patients. However, fees for collaboration among two or more licensees in a case or cases are permitted when properly disclosed.

- Reproduction or description in public of any psychological test or other assessment device, the value of which depends in whole or in part on the naiveté of the subject in ways that might invalidate the test or device.

VALUES of the THERAPIST

Therapists carry their own values and biases into sessions, which impact their therapeutic decisions, and are likely to influence the direction and outcome of the therapy. Therefore, to the extent possible, it is extremely important that the therapist:

1) Become aware of personal values and biases. Clarification of personal values is the first essential step;

2) Determine how these values and attitudes affect or interfere with clinical practice; and

3) Discuss with patients those values that are part of the treatment approach, whenever appropriate. For example, when working with a couple, it would be helpful to disclose your bias if you favor the couple staying together. Being clear and explicit about your bias will assist your patients. However, guard against inappropriately being directive on such issues as whether or not to divorce or separate, have a child, have an abortion, have an affair or sexual liaison, etc.

CONCLUSION

Ethical decision making is critical to the overall functioning of a psychotherapist. Ethical conflicts often involve issues of autonomy, respect, right to privacy, confidentiality, self-determination, and the obligation to protect and promote the welfare of a patient. A significantly compelling aspect to ethical decision making is the expectation that the problem solving process be explicit enough to bear public scrutiny.

When faced with an ethical conflict or issue, an initial determination as to the parameters of the situation and the issues involved is essential, as well as a review of ethical guidelines and legal standards, coupled with a focus on consequences, benefits, and risks (psychological, social and economic) associated with an array of alternative decisions. An analysis involving critical evaluation and intuitive response can begin to clarify the situation. Further exploration with a colleague, consultant, supervisor, or attorney is recommended.

In summary, ethical behavior in clinical practice is a dynamic and synergistic process. It results from an ongoing integration of didactic information acquired through one's academic and clinical education, an awareness of and working knowledge of professionally relevant ethics codes and standards of practice, and engagement in decision making and active problem solving methods. Added to this dynamic process is the therapist's personal traits and qualities of character, including maturity, awareness of limitations, knowledge of biases, responsibility, the capacity for informed judgment, compassion, and integrity. Hopefully, this review of issues will serve a small role in supporting your continued development as an ethical practitioner.

PART THREE:

VIGNETTE CONCEPTUALIZATION

This section is provided for clinicians wishing to conceptualize their potential responsibilities in the beginning stages of psychotherapy. It also serves the purpose of organizing responses for an oral presentation in a testing situation, such as for the oral licensing exam in psychology or marriage and family counseling. Both of these oral licensing exams provide a brief clinical vignette, followed by specific questions regarding a clinician's thought process in deciding to take a case, diagnostic impressions, assessments, treatment plans including goals and interventions for the particular diagnoses, and use of adjunctive services such as referrals, consultation, and supervision. This requires a certain level of comfort and familiarity with the process of thinking in a systematic and logical manner prior to speaking about the issues, as well as a strategy to articulate a comprehensive and accurate response. The following sections offers a variety of methods to use in these situations.

Accepting a Case

Whenever we read or hear a brief case vignette, one of the first determinations is whether it is appropriate for us to treat this particular individual, couple, family, or issue, and if it is within the scope of our practice and education, training, and experience. The decision will emerge after a thorough and systematic exploration of the two primary factors, discussed previously as Factors in Taking a Case: patient factors and psychotherapist factors

First, determine who the patient is, for example, if presented with a family, will you treat all members or the identified patient, or the couple. Next, explore the patient factors, then the therapist factors.

Therapist factors

This section requires an exploration of the therapist's scope of practice, education, training, professional experience, as well as abilities and limitations in treating this particular client, population, and issue. Any therapist issues and conflicts that could potentially interfere with the therapeutic process need to be addressed. Pope and Brown (1996) conceptualized two types of competence: intellectual competence and emotional competence. Intellectual competence is the knowledge and experiential base, including the assessment, treatment, and intervention skills possessed by the therapist. This area is traditionally encompassed by scope of education, training, and experience. Emotional competence refers to "the psychotherapist's ability to emotionally contain and tolerate the clinical material that emerges in treatment" (Koocher & Keith-Spiegel, 1998, p.55) and ability to assess bias, and engage in self care. This area is partly addressed by the reflection on countertransferential responses. The most important aspect here is articulating your limitations and knowing when you need to seek consultation or supervision.

Patient Factors in Taking the Case:

- Willingness
- Legally suitable
- Capacity

Psychotherapist Factors in Taking the Case

- Scope of practice
- Scope of education, training, experience
- Multiple relationships
- Unmanageable countertransference

If you determine that it is appropriate for you to accept the case based on a preliminary review of these initial items, then move on to the next section, addressing the issue or problem in depth.

Shadow

I have developed a mnemonic in honor of the goddess Mnemosyne, the goddess of memory, to assist in this process. *Mnemosyne* "to remember." Mnemonics comes from the Greek term *mnemonikos*, "of memory, mnemon, mindful. Pertaining to, aiding or intended to aid the memory" (Webster's New Riverside, 1984, p. 760). While Mnemosyne assists the therapist in this process of looking deeply within and under, she is also evoked for the patient, who is drawing on his or her oral history. I believe there is an art to memory, and have created categories with dramatic tones, but which represent continuums of experience or behavior: awareness of the continuum within each category, from a less to more serious progression of events, is best to keep in mind when conducting an assessment.

The mnemonic is: SHADOW - referring to the unseen, the hidden, or aspects not easily seen:

S	Suicide
H	Homicide
A	Abuse
D	Diversity
O	Organicity
W	Whole Person

Suicide

This category focuses on the range of behavior constituting danger to self. Active and immediate considerations involve the assessment of suicidal ideation and intent, including an expressed means and plan, past history of suicide attempts, level of hopelessness, the presence of support systems.

Homicide

This category focuses on danger to others, including the act of making serious threats of harm. This category allows for a sorting out of the clinician's responsibilities to warn an intended victim (Tarasoff duty to warn).

Abuse

Focuses on abuse, such as elder adult abuse, dependent adult abuse, child abuse. Mandated reporting duties are also addressed here.

Diversity

Focuses on the aspects of diversity which may remain hidden, unless inquired about. Another mnemonic is waiting in the wings: GRACE'S ODE: Gender role, religion, age, cultural context (including language), ethnicity, sexual orientation, developmental factors (individual, family life cycle), and economic (class issues) aspects.

Organicity

Pertaining to the body, such as physiological difficulties, neurological problems, substance use, eating disorders. Be certain to rule out any medical causes or conditions that may be contributing to the overall diagnostic picture.

Whole Person

Evoking a total view of the whole person in his or her humanness, not as a psychological or mental disorder, but a person within their full context and life situation, seen through a lens which includes their voice, behavior, thoughts, difficulties, strengths, coping capacities, and limitations. When you arrive at this section, go back to diversity to see if there is any issue likely to impact the provision of service, and address this clearly.

Strategies for Approaching Vignettes in an Oral Exam Context

Five Step Process

- 1. Acquisition
  Read the vignette comprehensively
- 2. Anxiety Management
  Active attention to breathing, being fully present in the moment, awareness of others in the room
- 3. Organization
  Use mnemonics. Allow Mnemosyne to guide you. The goddess of memory.
- 4. Presentation
  Practice with audience/tape
  Assess yourself for structure and style
- 5. Interaction
  Engage with the individuals in the room.

Acquisition

In this first step, one reads slowly, carefully, and thoroughly. Perhaps a second reading will assist you in comprehending the situation. First, obtain an overview of the situation, then look at specifics.

If you find that it's helpful to imagine the patient in front of you, do so. If you are an auditory learner, you may consider requesting permission to read the vignette aloud. You will usually read it once again for the tape recorder.

Organization

Use mnemonics to assist you in remembering information and providing a full response. The SHADOW mnemonic allows you to address any red flag issues that may be present. Red flag issues are issues which are considered priority items that should be addressed immediately early in the work.

There are certain points most skilled clinicians address immediately if they are presented in a vignette. These are often referred to as red flags, e.g., crisis and mandated reporting issues. Whenever addressing these issues, give full responses addressing the relevant legal standard or ethical issue that informs your practice.

One point on confidentiality. Please remember that it is the therapist's responsibility to hold confidential and safeguard information obtained in the therapy session. Deviations occur when they are necessary to avoid clear and imminent danger to the patient or others or when a mandate within the law takes precedence (e.g., Tarasoff duty to warn). One way to think of this is that responsibility for the decision that confidentiality must be breached rests solely on the therapist's judgment that the potential consequences of maintaining confidentiality are more onerous than if confidentiality were to be breached.

Initial Considerations: A SHADOW

A Accepting a case. Factors in Taking a case; patient and psychotherapist factors. Assess appropriateness for Treatment; e.g., age of Minor, and outpatient versus inpatient concerns.

S Suicide or Dangerousness to Self
H Homicide or Dangerousness to others
A Abuse (child, elder, spousal)
D Diversity Issues: Diversity lead us to another mnemonic: GRACE'S ODE (see below)
O Organicity; general medical conditions that may contribute to the focus of treatment; physiological concerns such as neurological disorders, drug or alcohol use and abuse, eating disorders
W Whole Person

GRACE'S ODE - in honor of the Three Graces in Greek mythology, considered to be the nature goddesses of gratitude.

DIVERSITY CONSIDERATIONS

G Gender, gender role
R Religion
A Age
C Cultural context, language
E Ethnicity (address any relevant acculturation issues)
S Sexual
O Orientation
D Developmental Stage, e.g., of life, or family
E Economic, or class context

Five Primary Elements in Vignette Response

I. Taking the Case
II. Who
III. What
IV. How
V. Other

1. Accepting the case
2. Who is patient?
3. What is the problem or the issue?
   Shadow, Grace's Ode, Clinical Assessment of issues including DSM IV diagnosis and developmental issues if relevant.
4. How will you intervene? Treatment plan, Interventions for issues, Include adjunctive services and referrals

What

What is the problem or issue What are the issues? (Assessment)

- What questions/issues do I need to discuss with this patient?
- What red flag issues are present? State the legal or ethical standards that inform your action.
- Are there safety issues that require action or my reporting to authorities?
- Clinical assessment of the issue using DSM IV Differential Diagnosis; Integrate the Mental Status Exam here if relevant to the vignette (Appearance, Behavior, Mood, Affect, Thought process and content, Perception, Insight); assess the developmental stage of the individual, couple, or family.

How

How do you intervene? What is the treatment?

- Develop the best treatment plan
- Indicate how you will treat the read flags mentioned under issues
- Present goals and interventions for the specific problems being treated. Goals are best stated as consensual goals (therapist and patient have agreed to these).
- Be sure to stay within your scope of practice and refer to others when necessary for making referrals
- Discuss short-term, intermediate, and long term treatment (if you were to work with the patient longer)

Other Issues

Case management issues can be addressed here, such as seeking adjunctive services in the interest of assisting the patient in meeting his or her goals.

- Are there any legal, ethical, or conflict of interest issues?
- Do I need to make any referrals to medical, social service, or legal personnel?

- How about adjunctive help such as self-help groups.
- Do I need to develop any therapeutic contracts that involve suicide or therapy commitments?
- What issues need to be discussed with my supervisor or with a consultant?

Presentation Style

Assessment

Structure your responses clearly and logically, for example:

I have a number of initial considerations in working with this case:

My first consideration is . . .
Another consideration is . . .

My primary diagnosis for this case is . . .
My secondary diagnosis is . . .

State what other information you would need in order to verify your speculations and make an appropriate assessment.

I have several concerns about this case.
If this, then . . .

This style focuses on each potential issue that is reasonably anticipated given the information within the vignette. If this is the diagnosis, then I would proceed in this manner. The goals may follow witht he interventions that will be used for each assessment area or identified issue.

Goals: State the short term, intermediate, and long-term goals, preferably consensual, co-created, and collaborative goals. Goals that take into account the patient's wishes.

When assessing, these are several discriminating questions to consider, in addition to red flags.

1. Are expected developmental crises present, such as adolescent rebellion, to which parents react abnormally? Is there a normal developmental crisis intensified by other stressors such as divorce, unemployment, illness, etc.?

2. Is the presenting problem new, or does it reflect a chronic situation? Chronic problems may reflect longer term characterological difficulties in individuals (personality disorders or stylistic characteristics). Acute problems may be due to recently occurring psychosocial stressors. An inquiry into precipitating factors is advised.

3. Can the presenting problems be seen as reflective of distress in a system? A family systems approach would consider one family member's problems as potentially representative of a systemic issue, e.g., a child's truancy indicating a difficulty at home or a substantial deterioration in a child's academic behavior, after successive episodes of domestic violence.

Interventions

Discuss possible interventions. How would you intervene in this situation, relative to the diagnosis and stated consensual goals. Comment on brief or short term goals first, such as addressing the crisis issues. Next discuss intermediate and possible longer term work.

1. Address all crisis situations first, then move on to longer term work with underlying issues.

2. Use fairly mainstream interventions, particularly those with empirically validated support. For example, if dysthymic disorder is the diagnosis, addressing safety issues, assessing the level of depression, and establish-

ing a therapeutic alliance is essential. Conducting an assessment for risk factors and the presence of suicidal ideation (intention, plan, means, previous attempts), and the strength of patient's support system, level of hopelessness, coping capacity, co-existing mental disorders or substance use, would all be necessary interventions, in addition to a referral to a physician and/or psychiatrist for a physical exam and medication evaluation.

For low risk situations, increasing the frequency of sessions, normalizing feelings, assisting the patient mobilize his or her support system, and agreeing to a no-suicide contract would be utilized.

For greater risk situations inpatient treatment (voluntary hospitalization is preferred, or involuntary if necessary) is explored. Intermediate goals may focus on the continued alleviation of symptoms. This may call for cognitive and behavioral interventions such as increasing coping skills and problem-solving abilities and addressing cognitions.

Longer term goals encompass the underlying factors that may contribute to the patient's vulnerability to depressive periods. Insight oriented approaches incorporating psychodynamic therapy and exploration of patient's inter and intrapersonal tendencies with group psychotherapy used as an adjunct could be helpful.

In terms of language, connect all your interventions directly with assessed problems. Make the connections with terms "because" and "in order to."

3. Acquiring more information is an important type of intervention. A clinical interview with a patient is a starting point, and collateral sources may provide additional information. Prior records from outpatient or inpatient psychotherapy, medical records, psychological

testing, and consultation with teachers are activities which can be very productive when attempting to engage in a comprehensive assessment.

Interaction with colleagues or examiners

During a case presentation or oral exam situation, the time devoted to questions and answers is pivotal. Some questions may focus on the diagnostic assessment requiring an articulation of the differential diagnostic process and how the diagnoses were reached. Others may focus on the treatment plan and interventions. Be willing to show your systematic thinking process as you describe the issues you rule out, stating your concerns, and how you address them. Providing comprehensive and thoughtful responses to the specific questions, without the addition of unnecessary tangential information is essential. Be willing to share current limitations and note situations where consultation or supervision would be sought. Above all maintain eye contact and acknowledge the other persons present in the room.

Therapist Self-Care

Therapist self-care is a complementary topic to ethics yet is considered innovative. Self-care incorporates a striving for emotional, psychological, physical, and spiritual well-being. This standard of self-care evolved from the theory that lack of self-care leads to ethical and legal transgressions, including boundary violations such as dual relationships (Lerman & Rigby, 1990). Recognizing or acknowledging personal limitations and seeking assistance when needed is a sign of strength, and can contribute to a therapist's growth and professionalism. Active engagement in self-care serves three primary functions: protects the patient by reducing risk factors, models growth and well-being, and protects the therapist against miscalculations and burn-out (Porter, 1995). The term *burnout* is associated with "fatique, frustration, or apathy resulting from prolonged stress, overwork, or intense activity" (Flexner, 1987, p. 281). Skorupa and Agresti (1993) noted that burnout can manifest as a "loss of empathy, respect, and positive feelings" (p. 281) toward patients.

The capacity for empathy is integral to this profession, as the capacity for self-care is essential to a therapist's emotional competence (Koocher & Keith-Spiegel, 1998). Emotional competence is required in order to successfully contain and tolerate difficult clinical material, and to become aware of those anxiety-provoking experiences that signal one's subtle transgressions. Engaging in personal psychotherapy or seeking consultation can refine or enhance one's ability to attend to these issues.

When the idea of reducing risk factors within a profession is raised, a practitioner may thoughtfully consider the legal risks and potential consequences of unethical or illegal behavior. While these are substantial and necessary to consider, there are a number of other risks associated within psychotherapy, primarily, the impact of this most intimate work on the values, worldview, and beliefs of the clinician.

Pearlman and Saakvitne (1995) developed the term *vicarious traumatization* to refer to therapists' inner responses and reactions to their work across time and across patients. Their focus was specifically on the therapist treating patients working through issues of incest. "We do not believe anyone, however psychologically healthy, can do this work and remain unchanged" (p. 295). Over the days, weeks, months, and years of doing this work, listening deeply, empathically engaging, containing uncomfortable material, confronting, and assisting with problem solving, the therapist is affected, over time, across patients. This impact on values, beliefs, and worldview can occur for therapists treating other populations as well. For some this results in a slow, debilitating disempowerment, for others a hubris, no longer seeking consultation from others, believing they have all the knowledge and insight needed to do the work successfully. Both of these extremes result in profound changes that can lead to unfavorable consequences, personally and professionally.

Active engagement in self-care can provide balance in one's life, improvement in personal relationships, and a renewed commitment to one's chosen vocation. An explicit focus on self-care integrates both the external and internal realities, such as relationships and activities with friends, family, and colleagues, in addition to involvement in spiritually, physically, and psychologically enriching endeavors, such as creative and artistic activities or appreciations, i.e., drawing, painting, writing, sculpting, dance, movement, drama, music, connecting with nature, contemplation, and meditation. Taking relaxing breaks from the intensity of the work, through vacations or leisure time can also be effective.

Self-care during oral exam preparation

When involved in a preparation process for an oral exam, a focus on self-care becomes indispensable. Attending to one's personal needs, exercise, making time for enjoyable activities, spending quality moments with friends and family, will all contribute to your preparation. Maintaining a sense of humor and creating play time can also be energizing. Adopting this integrative perspective will help manage your time. Reducing overall physical anxiety will decrease the additional physiological arousal that often accompanies test taking situations.

Procrastination is often a common defense against these fears, apprehensions, and anxieties. In fact, I have known many therapists who had spotless vehicles, well planted gardens, and extremely clean homes during their studying process! I have experience with these behaviors as well: I've taken graduate school comprehensive written and oral exams and two sets of licensing exams, one for my license to practice psychology, the other for marriage, family, and child counseling. If you find yourself engaging in these types of activities, acknowledge them as being within a normal range, allow yourself to engage in them, but perhaps on the principle where you promise yourself that activity after studying for a certain length of time. The paradoxical nature of this intervention might be one way to re-discover your motivation.

Using unique methods to directly limit, reduce, or minimize anxiety may be necessary, such as time limited studying, studying with a reliable partner, video or audiotaping yourself, relaxation training, guided imagery, dream work, behavioral rehearsal of the exam situation, biofeedback, and psychotherapy. And last, taking stock in all you already know will help you affirm your competence in this field. Remember that you have been successful in attaining your education and clinical experience up to this point. The task ahead is to enhance your skills to confidently articulate the depth and breadth of your current experience and knowledge. Hold positive intentions for yourself, express your appreciation and love for those who have supported you, and welcome the experience ahead as an opportunity for further growth and enrichment. For many it is experienced as an initiation process, moving across a threshold, into a profoundly meaningful and purposeful vocation. I wish you well in reaching this destination.

REFERENCES

Academy of Family Mediators. (1988). *Standards of Practice*. Lexington, MA: Author.

Ackerman, M. J., & Ackerman, M. (1997). Custody evaluation practices: A survey of experienced professionals (revisited). *Professional Psychology Research and Practice, 28*(2), 137-145.

American Counseling Association. (1988). *Ethical standards*. Alexandria, VA: Author.

American Psychological Association. (1992). Ethical principles of psychologists and code of conduct. *American Psychologist, 47*, 1597-1611.

American Psychological Association. (1993). Record keeping guidelines. *American Psychologist, 48*, 984-986.

American Psychological Association. (1994). Guidelines for child custody evaluations in divorce proceedings. *American Psychologist, 49*, 677-680.

Arons, G., & Spiegel, R. (1995). Unexpected encounters: The wizard of Oz exposed. In M. Sussman (Ed.), *A perilous calling: The hazards of psychotherapy practice* (pp. 125-138). New York: Wiley.

Association of Family and Conciliation Courts. (1995). *Model Standards of Practice for Child Custody Evaluations*. Madison, WI: Author.

Azar, S., & Siegel, B. (1990). Behavioral treatment of child abuse: A developmental perspective. *Behavior Modification, 14*, 279-300.

Beck, A., Resnick, Lettieri, D. (Eds.). (1986). *The prediction of suicide.* Philadelphia: Charles Press.

Beck, J. C. (1982). When the patient threatens violence: An empirical study after Tarasoff. *Bulletin of the American Academy of Psychiatry and Law, 10*, pp. 189-201.

Beebe, J. (1995). *Integrity in depth.* New York: Fromm International Publishing.

Berman, J. (1990). The problems of overlapping relationships in the political community. In H. Lerman & N. Porter (Eds.), Feminist ethics in psychotherapy (pp. 106-110). New York: Springer.

Biaggio, M., & Greene, B. (1995). Overlapping/dual relationships. In E. J. Rave & C. C. Larsen (Eds.), *Ethical decision making in therapy: Feminist perspectives* (pp. 88-123). New York: Guilford.

Bongar, B. (1991). *The suicidal patient.* Washington, DC: American Psychological Association.

Briere, J. (1989). *Therapy for adults molested as children: Beyond survival.* New York: Springer.

Briggs, K. C., & Myers, I. B. (1976). *Myers-Briggs Type Indicator.* Palo Alto, CA: Consulting Psychologists Press.

Brodsky, S. (1991). *Testifying in court: Guidelines and maxims for the expert witness.* Washington, DC: American Psychological Association.

California Department of Consumer Affairs. (1997). *Professional therapy never includes sex* (second edition). (One free copy available from DCA Publications, 401 S Street, Suite 100, 95814). <www.dca.ca.gov>

Caliso, J, & Milner, J. (1992). Childhood history of abuse and child abuse screening. *Child Abuse & Neglect, 16,* 647-659.

Canter, M. B., Bennett, B. E., Jones, S. E., & Nagy, T. F. (1994). *Ethics for psychologists: A commentary on the APA Ethics Code.* Washington, DC: American Psychological Association.

Casement, P. J. (1991). *Learning from the patient.* New York: Guilford.

Caudill, O.B., & Pope, K. (1995). *Law and mental health professionals: California.* Washington, DC: American Psychological Association.

Chemtob, C., Hamada, R., Bauer, G., Torigoe, R., & Kinney, B. (1988). Patient suicide: Frequency and impact on psychologists. *Professional Psychology: Research and Practice, 19,* 42-425.

Centers for Disease Control. (1997). Regional variations in suicide risk: United States 1990-1994. *Morbidity and Mortality Weekly Report, 46*(34): 789-793.

Conte, J., & Schuerman, J. (1987). Factors associated with an increased impact of child sexual abuse. *Child Abuse & Neglect, 11,* 201-211.

Crittenden, P., & Ainsworth, M. (1989). Child maltreatment and attachment theory. In D. Cicchetti & V. Carlson (Eds.), *Child maltreatment: Theory and research on the causes and consequences of child abuse and neglect* (pp. 432-463). New York: Cambridge University Press.

Factor, D., & Wolfe, D. (1990). Parental psychopathology and high-risk children. In R. Ammerman & M. Hersen (Eds.), *Children at risk: An evaluation of factors contributing to child abuse and neglect* (pp.171-198). New York: Plenum.

Feminist Therapy Institute. (1987). *Feminist therapy code of ethics.* Denver, CO: Author.

Flexner, S. (Ed.). (1987). *Random House dictionary of the English language* (2nd ed.). New York: Random House.

Friedrich, W., Grambsch, P., Broughton, D., Kuiper, J., & Beilke, R. (1991). Normative sexual behavior in children. *Pediatrics, 88*, 456-464.

Gates, K., & Speare, K. (1990). Overlapping relationships in rural communities. In H. Lerman & N. Porter (Eds.), *Feminist ethics in psychotherapy* (pp. 97-101). New York: Springer.

Gil, E., & Johnson, T. (1993). *Sexualized children: Assessment and treatment of sexualized children and children who molest.* Rockville, MD: Launch.

Gilligan, C. (1982). *In a different voice: Psychological theory and women's development.* Cambridge, MA: Harvard University.

Gottlieb, M. C. (1994). Ethical decision making, boundaries, and treatment effectiveness: A reprise. *Ethics and Behavior, 4*, 287-293.

Greenberg, S., & Shuman, D. (1997). Irreconcilable conflict between therapeutic and forensic roles. *Professional Psychology: Research and Practice, 28*(1), 50-57.

Grudin, R. (1990). *The grace of great things.* New York: Ticknor and Fields.

Guggenbuhl-Craig, A. (1995). Foreword. In L. Ross & M. Roy (Eds.), *Cast the first stone*. Wilmette, IL: Chiron.

Hall, J., & Hare-Mustin, R. (1983). Sanctions and the diversity of ethical complaints against psychologists. *American Psychologist, 38*, 714-729.

Hart, S., & Brassard, M. (1991). Psychological maltreatment: Progress achieved. *Development and Psychopathology, 3*, 61-70.

Hibbard, R., Ingersoll, G., & Orr, D. (1990). Behavior risk, emotional risk, and child abuse among adolescents in a nonclincial setting. *Pediatrics, 86*, 896-901.

Hill, M., Glaser, K., & Harden, J. (1995). A feminist model for ethical decision making. In E. Rave & C. Larsen (Eds.), *Ethical decision making in therapy: Feminist perspectives* (pp. 18-37). New York: Guilford.

Hoffman-Plotkin, D., & Twentyman, C. (1984). A multimodal assessment of behavioral and cognitive deficits in abused and neglected preschoolers. *Child Development, 55*, 794-802.

Hopkins, B. R., & Anderson, B. S. (1985). *The counselor and the law* (2nd ed.). Alexandria, VA: American Association for Counseling and Development.

Hunter, M, & Struve, J. (1998). *The ethical use of touch in psychotherapy.* Thousand Oaks, CA: Sage.

Johnston, J. R., & Campbell, L. E. (1993). Parent-child relationships in domestic violence families disputing custody. *Family and Conciliation Courts Review, 31*, 282-298.

Jung. C. G. (1954). Psychotherapy and a philosophy of life. In H. Read (Ed.) *The collected works* (R.F.C. Hull, Trans.) (Vol. 16). New Jersey: Princeton University Press. (Original work published 1943)

Jung, C. G. (1971). Psychological types. In H. Read (Ed.) *The collected works* (R.F.C. Hull, Trans.) (Vol. 6). New Jersey: Princeton University Press. (Original work published 1921)

Kaufman, J., & Zigler, E. (1987). Do abused children become abusive parents? *American Journal of Orthopsychiatry*, *57*, 186-192.

Kavanaugh, K., Youngblade, L., Reid, J., & Fagot, B. (1988). Interactions between children and abusive versus control parents. *Journal of Clinical Child Psychology*, *17*, 137-142.

Keith-Spiegel, P., & Koocher, G. (1985). *Ethics in psychology: professional standards and cases*. New York: Random House.

Kitchener, K. (1984). Intuition, critical evaluation and ethical principles: The foundation for ethical decisions in counseling psychology. *The Counseling Psychologist*, *12*(3), 43-55.

Kleespies, P., Penk, W., & Forsyth, J. (1993). The stress of patient suicidal behavior during clinical training: Incidence, impact, and recovery. *Professional Psychology: Research and Practice*, *24*(3), 293-303.

Kohlberg, L. (1981). *The philosophy of moral development.* San Francisco: Harper and Row.

Kohut. H. (1984). *How does analysis cure?* Chicago: University of Chicago Press.

Koocher, G., & Keith-Spiegel, P. (1998). *Ethics in psychology: Professional standards and cases* (2nd ed.). New York: Oxford University.

Lanktree, C., Briere, J., & Zaidi, J. (1991). Incidence and impact of sexual abuse in a child outpatient sample: The role of direct inquiry. *Child Abuse & Neglect, 15*, 447-453.

Lerman, H., & Rigby, D. (1990). Boundary violations: Misuse of the power of the therapist. In H. Lerman & N. Porter (Eds.), *Feminist ethics in psychotherapy* (pp. 51-59). New York: Springer.

Mills, D. (1984). Ethics education and adjudication within psychology. *American Psychologist, 39*(6), 669-675.

Milner, J. S. (1991). Physical child abuse perpetrator screening and evaluation. *Criminal Justice and Behavior, 18*, 47-63.

Milner, J.S., & Chilamkurti, C. (1991). Physical child abuse perpetrator characteristics: A review of the literature. *Journal of Interpersonal Violence, 6*, 345-366.

Moustakas, C. (1990). *Heuristic research: Design, methodology, and applications*. Newbury Park: Sage.

O'Neill, P. (1998). *Negotiating consent in psychotherapy*. New York: New York University Press.

Office of the Attorney General. (June 28, 1984). *Opinion of John K. Van De Kamp, Attorney General. No. 83-810*. Sacramento, CA: Office of the Attorney General.

Olin, J., & Keatinge, C. (1998). *Rapid psychological assessment*. New York: John Wiley.

Oxford dictionary of English etymology. (1966). New York: Oxford University Press.

Pearlman, L. A., & Saakvitne, K. W. (1995). The therapeutic relationship as the context for countertransference and vicarious traumatization. In *Trauma and the therapist* (pp. 15-34). New York: W. W. Norton.

Pope, K. (1991). Dual relationships in psychotherapy. *Ethics and Behavior, 1*, 21-34.

Pope, K., & Bajt, T. (1988). When laws and values conflict: A dilemma for psychologists. *American Psychologist, 43*, 828.

Pope, K., & Bouhoutsos, J. (1986). *Sexual intimacy between therapists and patients.* New York: Praeger.

Pope, K., & Brown, L. (1996). *Recovered memories of abuse: Assessment, therapy, forensics.* Washington, DC: American Psychological Association.

Pope, K., Tabachnick, B., & Keith-Spiegel, P. (1987). Ethics of practice: The beliefs and behaviors of psychologists as therapists. *American Psychologist, 42*, 993-1006.

Pope, K., & Vasquez, M. (1991). *Ethics in psychotherapy and counseling: A practical guide for psychologists.* San Francisco: Jossey-Bass.

Pope, K., & Vasquez, M. (1998). *Ethics in psychotherapy and counseling: A practical guide*. San Francisco: Jossey-Bass.

Porter, N. (1995). Therapist self-care: A proactive ethical approach. In H. Lerman & N. Porter (Eds.), *Feminist ethics in psychotherapy* (pp. 247-266). New York: Springer.

Resnik, H. (1980). Suicide. In H. Kaplan & B. Sadock (Eds.), *Comprehensive textbook of psychiatry* (3rd ed.). Baltimore, MD: Williams & Wilkins.

Rilke, R. M. (1984). *Letters to a young poet.* (S. Mitchell, Trans.). New York: Random House.

Rohner, R., & Rohner, E. (1980). Antecedents and consequences of parental rejection: A theory of emotional abuse. *Child Abuse & Neglect, 4*, 189-198.

Rosenberg, J. (1999). Suicide prevention: An integrated training model using affective and action-based interventions. *Professional Psychology: Research and Practice, 30*(1), 83-87.

Salgo v. Stanford University. (1957). 317 P2d 170 (California Court of Appeal).

Schneidman, E. (1975). *Suicidology: Contemporary developments.* New York: Grune & Stratton.

Schneidman, E. (1993). Some controversies in suicidology: Toward a mentalistic discipline. *Suicide and Life-Threatening Behavior, 23*(4), 292-298.

Schutz, B. (1982). *Legal liability to psychotherapy.* San Francisco: Jossey-Bass.

Sears, V. (1990). On being an "only" one. In H. Lerman & N. Porter (Eds.), *Feminist ethics in psychotherapy* (pp. 102-105). New York: Springer.

Shengold, L. (1979). Child abuse and deprivation: Soul murder. *Journal of the American Psychoanalytic Association, 27,* 533-599.

Singer, M., Petchers, M., & Hussey, D. (1989). The

relationship between sexual abuse and substance abuse among psychiatrically hospitalized adolescents. *Child Abuse & Neglect, 13*, 319-325.

Skorupa, J., & Agresti, A. (1993). Ethical beliefs about burnout and continued professional practice. *Professional Psychology: Research and Practice, 24*(3), 281-285.

Smith, A. (1990). Working within the lesbian community: The dilemma of overlapping relationships. In H. Lerman & N. Porter (Eds.), *Feminist ethics in psychotherapy* (pp. 92-96). New York: Springer.

Sommers-Flanagan, J., & Sommers-Flanagan, R. (1995). Intake interviewing with suicidal patients: A systematic approach. *Professional Psychology: Research and Practice, 26*(1), 41-47.

Tarasoff v. Board of Regents of the University of California, Cal. Rptr. 14, No. S.F. 23042 (Cal. Sup. Ct., July 1, 1976) 131.

Trickett, P., & Kuczynski, L. (1986). Children's misbehaviors and parental discipline strategies in abusive and nonabusive families. *Developmental Psychology, 27*, 148-158.

Tymchuk, A. (1986). Guidelines for ethical decision making. *Canadian Psychology, 27*, 36-43.

van der Kolk, B., Perry, J., & Herman, J. (1991). Childhood origins of self-destructive behavior. *American Journal of Psychiatry, 148*, 1665-1671.

VandeCreek, L., & Knapp, S. (1993). *Tarasoff and beyond: Legal and clinical considerations in the treatment of life-endangering patients.* Sarasota, FL: Professional Resource Press.

Webster's II New Riverside University Dictionary. (1984). Boston, MA: Houghton Mifflin.

Widom, C. (1989). Does violence beget violence? A critical examination of the literature. *Psychological Bulletin, 106*, 3-28.

Zwillich, T. (1998). Risk factors for suicide in children. *Clinical Psychiatry News, 26*(6):18.

APPENDIX A: RESOURCES

Academy of Family Mediators. Non-profit educational membership association. Members provide mediation services to families facing decisions involving separation, marital dissolution, child custody, parenting, visitation, property division, wills and estates, elder care, spousal support, child support, prenuptial agreements. Annual conference, mediator referrals, and educational materials. 5 Militia Drive, Lexington, MA 02421. Phone (781) 674-2663. <www.mediators.org>

Adults Molested as Children United (AMAC). Referral source. Groups for all sexual abuse survivors; national referrals. PO Box 952, San Jose, CA 95108. <www.movingforward.org>

American Association for Protecting Children, American Humane Assn. National center promotes responsive child protection services in every community through program planning, training, education, and consultation. 63 Inverness Drive East, Englewood, CO 80112-5117. 1(800)227-4645. <www.americanhumane.org>

American Association of Sex Educators, Counselors, and Therapists. A not-for-profit professional organization providing certification. Members include health professionals, clergy, researchers, students, and lawyers. Promotes understanding of human sexuality and healthy sexual behavior. Continuing education and conference. Box 238, Mount Vernon, IA 52314. Fax: (319) 895-6203. E-mail: aasect@worldnet.att.net <www.aasect.org>

American Medical Association. Department of Mental Health. Provides referrals related to family violence and child abuse. Brochures on diagnosis, treatment, and medicolegal issues concerning child abuse. 515 State Street, Chicago, IL 60610. (312) 464-5066. <www.ama.org>

American Professional Society on the Abuse of Children. (APSAC). Organization for professionals in the field of child abuse treatment and prevention; offers advocacy, information, guidelines, referral services to professionals working in the field. Journal of Child Maltreatment. 332 S. Michigan Ave., Suite 1600, Chicago, IL 60604. (312) 554-0166. <www.apsac.org>

American Psychological Association. Professional association for psychologists. Many excellent journals of interest to mental health professionals, e.g., American Psychologist, Professional Psychology: Research and Practice, holds yearly conference, monthly newsletter: The APA Monitor. 750 First St., N.E., Washington, DC 20002. Phone: (202) 336-5500. <www.apa.org>

Board of Behavioral Sciences, California. Licensing organization for marriage and family therapists, social workers, educational psychologists. Consumer protection through the regulation of licensees, interns, associates, and corporations. 400 R Street, Suite 3150, Sacramento, CA 95814. (916) 445-4933. <www.bbs.ca.gov>

Board of Psychology, California. State licensing organization for psychologists. Committed to protection of the health, safety, and welfare of consumers of psychological services.1422 Howe Avenue, Suite 22, Sacramento, 95825. (916) 263-2699. <www.dca.ca.gov/psych/>

California Association for Marriage and Family Therapists. Professional association for marriage, family, and child counselors. Members include students, trainees, and interns. Journal: The California Therapist. 7901 Raytheon Road, San Diego, CA 92111-1606. (619) 292-2638. <www.camft.org>

California Codes. Up to date information on the various California Codes relevant to the practice of psychotherapy may be viewed on the website: <www.leginfo.ca.gov>

California Psychological Association. Pofessional association for licensed psychologists and others affiliated with the delivery of psychological services. Low-cost memberships for students. Conferences and monthly newsletter. 1022 "G" Street, Sacramento, CA 95814-0817. Phone: 916-325-9786 Fax: 916-325-9790. <www.calpsychlink.org>

Child Survivor of Traumatic Stress. Electronic version of a newsletter for professionals who work with traumatized children. Articles include specialized assessments and scales for assessing post-traumatic responses. <www.ummed.edu/pub/k/kfletche/kidsurv.html>

Childhelp USA - National Hot Line: (800) 422-4453. Offers a 24-hour crisis hot line, information, referral network for support groups and therapists, and reporting suspected abuse. Sponsors Adult Survivors of Child Abuse Anonymous meetings. c/o NSCAAP, PO Box 630, Hollywood, CA 90028. <www.childhelpusa.org>

Domestic Abuse Intervention Project (Duluth). A National information center. Provides information on domestic abuse including batterers' treatment information. (218) 722-2781.

Family Resource Coalition. Membership organization of social service agencies concerned with strengthening families through preventive services. Maintains a clearinghouse for information on family resource programs, quarterly newsletter. 200 S. Michigan Avenue, 16th Floor, Chicago, IL 60604. (312) 341-0900. <www.frca.org>

Family Violence Prevention Fund. National non-profit organization that focuses on domestic violence education, prevention, and public policy reform. <www.lgc.org/fund>

Feminist Therapy Institute. Promulgate the Ethical Guidelines for Feminist Therapists. Includes the integral significance of diversity and anti-racism. Feminist Therapy Institute, Inc., Corporate Office: 50 Steele Street, #850, Denver, CO 80209.

Incest Survivor Information Exchange (ISIE). Newsletter for survivors' writings, art work, & exchange of information. PO Box 3399, New Haven, CT 06515. (203) 389-5166.

Incest Survivors Resource Network International: Information and networking for survivors. PO Box 7375, Las Cruces, NM 88006-7375. (505) 521-4260. <www.zianet.com/ISRNI/>

International Critical Incident Stress Foundation, Inc. Educational organization providing national trainings for professionals. Critical Incident Stress Debriefing Model. 5018 Dorsey Hall Drive, Suite 104, Ellicot, MD 21042. (410) 750-9600. <www.icisf.org>

International Society for the Study of MPD and Dissociative Disorders: Educational organization; conferences, literature. 60 Revere Drive, Suite 500, Northbrook, IL 60062. (708) 966-4322. <www.issd.org>

International Society for Traumatic Stress Studies. Professional association. Journal of Traumatic Stress and monthly newsletter. 60 Revere Drive, Suite 500, Northbrook, IL 60062 (312) 644-0828. <www.istss.org>

MALE: Publishes men's issues forum for male survivors. PO Box 380181, Denver, CO 80238-1181. (303) 320-4365. <www.malesurvivor.org>

National Board for Certified Counselors, Inc. Professional certification board which certifies counselors as having met standards for the general and specialty practice of professional counseling established by the Board. 3 Terrace Way, Suite D, Greensboro, NC 27403-3660. <www.nbcc.org>

National Center for Missing and Exploited Children. National clearinghouse and resource center. Funded by U.S. Department of Justice. Provides free single copies of useful publications. 2101 Wilson Blvd., Suite 550, Arlington, VA 22201. (703) 235-3900. <www.ncmec.org>

National Center for the Prosecution of Child Abuse. American Prosecutors Research Institute. Legal clearinghouse, literature, research, and professional workshops. 1033 N. Fairfax St., Suite 200, Alexandria, VA 22314. (703) 739-0321. <www.ncjrs.org>

National Center on Elder Abuse and Neglect. NCEA produces biannual compilations of state adult protective services data, and helped conduct the National Elder Abuse Incidence Study. <www.gwjapan.com/NCEA>

National Clearinghouse for Alcohol and Drug Information. A communications service of the Center for Substance Abuse Prevention. Provides information on research, publications, prevention and education resources, and prevention programs, and a catalog. 11426 Rockville Pike, Suite 200, Rockville, MD 20852. (800) 729-6686. <www.health.org>

National Clearinghouse on Child Abuse and Neglect Information (NCCAN). U.S. Department of Health and Human Services. For professionals seeking information on prevention, identification, and treatment of child abuse, neglect, and related welfare issues. P.O. Box 1182, Washington, DC 20012. (703) 385-7565.<www.calib.com/nccanch>

National Clearinghouse on Families and Youth (NCFY). Tailors research to meet the needs of organizations, programs or communities; links people with others facing similar challenges in their work or who have creative ideas about improving youth practice and policy; provides updates on youth initiatives. P.O. Box 13505, Silver Spring, MD 20911-3505. (301) 608-8098. <www.ncfy.com>

National Coalition Against Domestic Violence. National organization that works to end violence in the lives of families. Information, technical assistance, publications, newsletters, and resource materials. P.O. Box 18749, Denver, CO 80218. (303) 839-1852. <www.ncadv.org>

National Coalition Against Sexual Assault. Advocacy, education, and public policy information. 125 N. Enola Drive, Enola, PA 17025. (717) 728-9764. <ncasa.org>

National Committee to Prevent Child Abuse (NCPCA): Information and referral. Educational materials on parenting and child abuse prevention. Annual national survey. Free catalog: (800)835-2671. 206 S. Michigan Ave, 17th Floor, Chicago, IL 60604-4357. (312) 663-3520. <www.childabuse.org>

National Organization for Victim Assistance. (NOVA). Wash., DC. Information, Referral, Community Crisis Response Assistance Training. (800) 879-6682. <www.try-nova.org>

Parents United International (and Daughters and Sons United): Dedicated to the assistance of children, parents, & adults molested as children, and others concerned with child sexual abuse & related problems. PO Box 952, San Jose, CA 95108-0952. (408) 453-7616; Crisis line: (408) 279-8228. <www.giarretto.org>

People of Color Leadership Institute. Goals are to improve cultural competence in child welfare systems that serve children and families of color. Institute has developed a cultural competence training guide and bibliography of publications about child welfare as it relates to people of color. 714 G St., SE, Washington, DC 20003. (202) 544-3144.

Survivors of Incest Anonymous: International network of self-help meetings, literature, pen pals, speakers, meeting information, and bi-monthly bulletin. SASE (two stamps) for information about support groups. World Service Office: PO Box 21817, Baltimore, MD 21222-6817. (410) 282-3400. <selfin.org/survivor/survorgs.1.html>

The Healing Woman: Publishes monthly newsletter for women recovering from childhood sexual abuse. PO Box 3038, Moss Beach, CA 94038-3038. (415) 728-0339. <www.healingwoman.org>

VOICES in Action (Victims of Incest Can Emerge Survivors): International organization for survivors and partners ("pro-survivors"). Conferences, special interest groups, & newsletter. PO Box 148309, Chicago, IL 60614. (773) 327-1500. (800) 7-VOICE-8 <www.voices-action.g

Appendix B

Ethical Principles of Psychologists and Code of Conduct

Contents

1.21 Third-Party Requests for Services
1.22 Delegation to and Supervision of Subordinates
1.23 Documentation of Professional and Scientific Work
1.24 Records and Data
1.25 Fees and Financial Arrangements
1.26 Accuracy in Reports to Payors and Funding Sources
1.27 Referrals and Fees

2. Evaluation, Assessment, or Intervention
2.0 Evaluation, Diagnosis, and Interventions in Professional Context
2.02 Competence and Appropriate Use of Assessments and Interventions
2.03 Test Construction
2.04 Use of Assessment in General and With Special Populations
2.05 Interpreting Assessment Results
2.06 Unqualified Persons
2.07 Obsolete Tests and Outdated Test Results
2.08 Test Scoring and Interpretation Services
2.09 Explaining Assessment Results
2.10 Maintaining Test Security

3. Advertising and Other Public Statements
3.01 Definition of Public Statements
3.02 Statements by Others
3.03 Avoidance of False or Deceptive Statements
3.04 Media Presentations
3.05 Testimonials
3.06 In-Person Solicitation

4. Therapy
4.01 Structuring the Relationship
4.02 Informed Consent to Therapy
4.03 Couple and Family Relationships
4.04 Providing Mental Health Services to Those Served by Others
4.05 Sexual Intimacies With Current Patients or Clients
4.06 Therapy With Former Sexual Partners
4.07 Sexual Intimacies With Former Therapy Patients
4.08 Interruption of Services
4.09 Terminating the Professional Relationship

5. PRIVACY AND CONFIDENTIALITY
5.01 Discussing the Limits of Confidentiality
5.02 Maintaining Confidentiality
5.03 Minimizing Intrusions on Privacy
5.04 Maintenance of Records
5.05 Disclosures
5.06 Consultations
5.07 Confidential Information in Databases
5.08 Use of Confidential Information for Didactic or Other Purposes
5.09 Preserving Records and Data
5.10 Ownership of Records and Data
5.11 Withholding Records for Nonpayment

6. Teaching, Training, Supervision, Research, and Publishing
6.01 Design of Education and Training Programs
6.02 Descriptions of Education and Training Programs
6.03 Accuracy and Objectivity in Teaching
6.04 Limitation on Teaching
6.05 Assessing Student and Supervisee Performance
6.06 Planning Research
6.07 Responsibility
6.08 Compliance With Law and Standards
6.09 Institutional Approval
6.10 Research Responsibilities
6.11 Informed Consent to Research
6.12 Dispensing With Informed Consent
6.13 Informed Consent in Research Filming or Recording
6.14 Offering Inducements for Research Participants
6.15 Deception in Research
6.16 Sharing and Utilizing Data
6.17 Minimizing Invasiveness
6.18 Providing Participants With Information About the Study
6.19 Honoring Commitments
6.20 Care and Use of Animals in Research
6.21 Reporting of Results
6.22 Plagiarism
6.23 Publication Credit
6.24 Duplicate Publication of Data
6.25 Sharing Data
6.26 Professional Reviewers

INTRODUCTION

The American Psychological Association's (APA's) Ethical Principles of Psychologists and Code of Conduct (hereinafter referred to as the Ethics Code) consists of an Introduction, a Preamble, six General Principles (A - F), and specific Ethical Standards. The Introduction discusses the intent, organization, procedural considerations, and scope of application of the Ethics Code. The Preamble and General Principles are aspirational goals to guide psychologists toward the highest ideals of psychology. Although the Preamble and General Principles are not themselves enforceable rules, they should be considered by psychologists in arriving at an ethical course of action and may be considered by ethics bodies in interpreting the Ethical Standards. The Ethical Standards set forth enforceable rules for conduct as psychologists. Most of the Ethical Standards are written broadly, in order to apply to psychologists in varied roles, although the application of an Ethical Standard may vary depending on the context. The Ethical Standards are not exhaustive. The fact that a given conduct is not specifically addressed by the Ethics Code does not mean that it is necessarily either ethical or unethical.

Membership in the APA commits members to adhere to the APA Ethics Code and to the rules and procedures used to implement it. Psychologists and students, whether or not they are APA members, should be aware that the Ethics Code may be applied to them by state psychology boards, courts, or other public bodies.

This Ethics Code applies only to psychologists' work-related activities, that is, activities that are part of the psychologists' scientific and professional functions or that are psychological in nature. It includes the clinical or counseling practice of psychology, research, teaching, supervision of trainees, development of assessment instruments, conducting assessments, educational counseling, organizational consulting, social intervention, administration, and other activities as well. These work-related activities can be distinguished from the purely private conduct of a psychologist, which ordinarily is not within the purview of the Ethics Code.

The Ethics Code is intended to provide standards of professional conduct that can be applied by the APA and by other bodies that choose to adopt them. Whether or not a psychologist has violated the Ethics Code does not by itself determine whether he or she is legally liable in a court action, whether a contract is enforceable, or whether other legal consequences occur. These results are based on legal rather than ethical rules. However, compliance with or violation of the Ethics Code may be admissible as evidence in some legal proceedings, depending on the circumstances.

In the process of making decisions regarding their professional behavior, psychologists must consider this Ethics Code, in addition to applicable laws and psychology board regulations. If the Ethics Code establishes a higher standard of conduct than is required by law, psychologists must meet the higher ethical standard. If the Ethics Code standard appears to conflict with the requirements of law, then psychologists make known their commitment to the Ethics Code and take steps to resolve the conflict in a responsible manner. If neither law nor the Ethics Code resolves an issue, psychologists should consider other professional materials (Footnote 1) and the dictates of their own conscience, as well as seek consultation with others within the field when this is practical.

The procedures for filing, investigating, and resolving complaints of unethical conduct are described in the current Rules and Procedures of the APA Ethics Committee. The actions that APA may take for violations of the Ethics Code include actions such as reprimand, censure, termination of APA membership, and referral of the matter to other bodies. Complainants who seek remedies such as monetary damages in alleging ethical violations by a psychologist must resort to private negotiation, administrative bodies, or the courts. Actions that violate the Ethics Code may lead to the imposition of sanctions on a psychologist by bodies other than APA, including state psychological associations, other professional groups, psychology boards, other state or federal agencies, and payors for health services. In addition to actions for violation of the Ethics Code, the APA Bylaws provide that APA may take action against a member after his or her conviction of a felony, expulsion or suspension from an affiliated state psychological association, or suspension or loss of licensure.

PREAMBLE

Psychologists work to develop a valid and reliable body of scientific knowledge based on research. They may apply that knowledge to human behavior in a variety of contexts. In doing so, they perform many roles, such as researcher, educator, diagnostician, therapist, supervisor, consultant, administrator, social interventionist, and expert witness. Their goal is to broaden knowledge of behavior and, where appropriate, to apply it pragmatically to improve the condition of both the individual and society. Psychologists respect the central importance of freedom of inquiry and expression in research, teaching, and publication. They also strive to help the public in developing informed judgments and choices concerning human behavior. This Ethics Code provides a common set of values upon which psychologists build their professional and scientific work.

This Code is intended to provide both the general principles and the decision rules to cover most situations encountered by psychologists. It has as its primary goal the welfare and protection of the individuals and groups with whom psychologists work. It is the individual responsibility of each psychologist to aspire to the highest possible standards of conduct. Psychologists respect and protect human and civil rights, and do not knowingly participate in or condone unfair discriminatory practices.

The development of a dynamic set of ethical standards for a psychologist's work-related conduct requires a personal commitment to a lifelong effort to act ethically; to encourage ethical behavior by students, supervisees, employees, and colleagues, as appropriate; and to consult with others, as needed, concerning ethical problems. Each psychologist supplements, but does not violate, the Ethics Code's values and rules on the basis of guidance drawn from personal values, culture, and experience.

GENERAL PRINCIPLES

Principle A: Competence

Psychologists strive to maintain high standards of competence in their work. They recognize the boundaries of their particular competencies and the limitations of their expertise. They provide only those services and use only those techniques for which they are qualified by education, training, or experience. Psychologists are cognizant of the fact that the competencies required in serving, teaching, and/or studying groups of people vary with the distinctive characteristics of those groups. In those areas in which recognized professional standards do not yet exist, psychologists exercise careful judgment and take appropriate precautions to protect the welfare of those with whom they work. They maintain knowledge of relevant scientific and professional information related to the services they render, and they recognize the need for ongoing education. Psychologists make appropriate use of scientific, professional, technical, and administrative resources.

Principle B: Integrity

Psychologists seek to promote integrity in the science, teaching, and practice of psychology. In these activities psychologists are honest, fair, and respectful of others. In describing or reporting their qualifications, services, products, fees, research, or teaching, they do not make statements that are false, misleading, or deceptive. Psychologists strive to be aware of their own belief systems, values, needs, and limitations and the effect of these on their work. To the extent feasible, they attempt to clarify for relevant parties the roles they are performing and to function appropriately in accordance with those roles. Psychologists avoid improper and potentially harmful dual relationships.

Principle C: Professional and Scientific Responsibility

Psychologists uphold professional standards of conduct, clarify their professional roles and obligations, accept appropriate responsibility for their behavior, and adapt their methods to the needs of different populations. Psychologists consult with, refer to, or cooperate with other professionals and institutions to the extent needed to serve the best interests of their patients, clients, or other recipients of their services. Psychologists' moral standards and conduct are personal matters to the same degree as is true for any other person, except as psychologists' conduct may compromise their professional responsibilities or reduce the public's trust in psychology and psychologists. Psychologists are concerned about the ethical compliance of their colleague's scientific and professional conduct. When appropriate, they consult with colleagues in order to prevent or avoid unethical conduct.

Principle D: Respect for People's Rights and Dignity

Psychologists accord appropriate respect to the fundamental rights, dignity, and worth of all people. They respect the rights of individuals to privacy, confidentiality, self-determination, and autonomy, mindful that legal and other obligations may lead to inconsistency and conflict with the exercise of these rights. Psychologists are aware of cultural, individual, and role differences, including those due to age, gender, race, ethnicity, national origin, religion, sexual orientation, disability, language, and socioeconomic status. Psychologists try to eliminate the effect on their work of biases based on those factors, and they do not knowingly participate in or condone unfair discriminatory practices.

Principle E: Concern for Others' Welfare

Psychologists seek to contribute to the welfare of those with whom they interact professionally. In their professional actions, psychologists weigh the welfare and rights of their patients or clients, students, supervisees, human research participants, and other affected persons, and the welfare of animal subjects of research. When conflicts occur among psychologists' obligations or concerns, they attempt to resolve these conflicts and to perform their roles in a responsible fashion that avoids or minimizes harm. Psychologists are sensitive to real and ascribed differences in power between themselves and others, and they do not exploit or mislead other people during or after professional relationships.

Principle F: Social Responsibility

Psychologists are aware of their professional and scientific responsibilities to the community and the society in which they work and live. They apply and make public their knowledge of psychology in order to contribute to human welfare. Psychologists are concerned about and work to mitigate the causes of human suffering. When undertaking research, they strive to advance human welfare and the science of psychology. Psychologists try to avoid misuse of their work. Psychologists comply with the law and encourage the development of law and social policy that serve the interests of their patients and clients and the public. They are encouraged to contribute a portion of their professional time for little or no personal advantage.

ETHICAL STANDARDS

1. General Standards

These General Standards are potentially applicable to the professional and scientific activities of all psychologists.

1.01 Applicability of the Ethics Code.

The activity of a psychologist subject to the Ethics Code may be reviewed under these Ethical Standards only if the activity is part of his or her work-related functions or the activity is psychological in nature. Personal activities having no connection to or effect on psychological roles are not subject to the Ethics Code.

1.02 Relationship of Ethics and Law.

If psychologists' ethical responsibilities conflict with law, psychologists make known their commitment to the Ethics Code and take steps to resolve the conflict in a responsible manner.

1.03 Professional and Scientific Relationship.

Psychologists provide diagnostic, therapeutic, teaching, research, supervisory, consultative, or other psychological services only in the context of a defined professional or scientific relationship or role. (See also Standards 2.01, Evaluation, Diagnosis, and Interventions in Professional Context, and 7.02, Forensic Assessments.)

1.04 Boundaries of Competence.

(a) Psychologists provide services, teach, and conduct research only within the boundaries of their competence, based on their education, training, supervised experience, or appropriate professional experience.

(b) Psychologists provide services, teach, or conduct research in new areas or involving new techniques only after first undertaking appropriate study, training, supervision, and/or consultation from persons who are competent in those areas or techniques.

(c) In those emerging areas in which generally recognized standards for preparatory training do not yet exist, psychologists nevertheless take reasonable steps to ensure the competence of their work and to protect patients, clients, students, research participants, and others from harm.

1.05 Maintaining Expertise.
Psychologists who engage in assessment, therapy, teaching, research, organizational consulting, or other professional activities maintain a reasonable level of awareness of current scientific and professional information in their fields of activity, and undertake ongoing efforts to maintain competence in the skills they use.

1.06 Basis for Scientific and Professional Judgments.
Psychologists rely on scientifically and professionally derived knowledge when making scientific or professional judgments or when engaging in scholarly or professional endeavors.

1.07 Describing the Nature and Results of Psychological Services.
(a) When psychologists provide assessment, evaluation, treatment, counseling, supervision, teaching, consultation, research, or other psychological services to an individual, a group, or an organization, they provide, using language that is reasonably understandable to the recipient of those services, appropriate in- formation beforehand about the nature of such services and appropriate information later about results and conclusions. (See also Standard 2.09, Explaining Assessment Results.)
(b) If psychologists will be precluded by law or by organizational roles from providing such information to particular individuals or groups, they so inform those individuals or groups at

the outset of the service.

1.08 Human Differences.

Where differences of age, gender, race, ethnicity, national origin, religion, sexual orientation, disability, language, or socioeconomic status significantly affect psychologists' work concerning particular individuals or groups, psychologists obtain the training, experience, consultation, or supervision necessary to ensure the competence of their services, or they make appropriate referrals.

1.09 Respecting Others.

In their work-related activities, psychologists respect the rights of others to hold values, attitudes, and opinions that differ from their own.

1.10 Nondiscrimination.

In their work-related activities, psychologists do not engage in unfair discrimination based on age, gender, race, ethnicity, national origin, religion, sexual orientation, disability, socioeconomic status, or any basis proscribed by law.

1.11 Sexual Harassment.

(a) Psychologists do not engage in sexual harassment. Sexual harassment is sexual solicitation, physical advances, or verbal or nonverbal conduct that is sexual in nature, that occurs in connection with the psychologist's activities or roles as a psychologist, and that either: (1) is unwelcome, is offensive, or creates a hostile workplace environment, and the psychologist knows or is told this; or (2) is sufficiently severe or intense to be abusive to a reasonable person in the context. Sexual harassment can consist of a single intense or severe act or of multiple persistent or pervasive acts.

(b) Psychologists accord sexual-harassment complainants and respondents dignity and respect. Psychologists do not participate in denying a person academic admittance or advancement, employment, tenure, or promotion, based solely upon their having made, or their being the subject of, sexual harassment charges. This does not preclude taking action based upon the outcome of such proceedings or consideration of other appropriate information.

1.12 Other Harassment.

Psychologists do not knowingly engage in behavior that is harassing or demeaning to persons with whom they interact in their work based on factors such as those persons' age, gender, race, ethnicity, national origin, religion, sexual orientation, disability, language, or socioeconomic status.

1.13 Personal Problems and Conflicts.

(a) Psychologists recognize that their personal problems and conflicts may interfere with their effectiveness. Accordingly, they refrain from undertaking an activity when they know or should know that their personal problems are likely to lead to harm to a patient, client, colleague, student, research participant, or other person to whom they may owe a professional or scientific obligation.

(b) In addition, psychologists have an obligation to be alert to signs of, and to obtain assistance for, their personal problems at an early stage, in order to prevent significantly impaired performance.

(c) When psychologists become aware of personal problems that may interfere with their performing work-related duties adequately, they take appropriate measures, such as obtaining professional consultation or assistance, and determine whether they should limit, suspend, or terminate their work-related duties.

1.14 Avoiding Harm.

Psychologists take reasonable steps to avoid harming their patients or clients, research participants, students, and others with whom they work, and to minimize harm where it is foreseeable and unavoidable.

1.15 Misuse of Psychologists' Influence.

Because psychologists' scientific and professional judgments and actions may affect the lives of others, they are alert to and guard against personal, financial, social, organizational, or political factors that might lead to misuse of their influence.

1.16 Misuse of Psychologists' Work.

(a) Psychologists do not participate in activities in which it appears likely that their skills or data will be misused by others, unless corrective mechanisms are available. (See also Standard 7.04, Truthfulness and Candor.)

(b) If psychologists learn of misuse or misrepresentation of their work, they take reasonable steps to correct or minimize the misuse or misrepresentation.

1.17 Multiple Relationships.

(a) In many communities and situations, it may not be feasible or reasonable for psychologists to avoid social or other nonprofessional contacts with persons such as patients, clients, students, supervisees, or research participants. Psychologists must always be sensitive to the potential harmful effects of other contacts on their work and on those persons with whom they deal. A psychologist refrains from entering into or promising another personal, scientific, professional, financial, or other relationship with such persons if it appears likely that such a relationship reasonably might impair the psychologist's objectivity or otherwise interfere with the psychologist's effectively performing his or her functions as a psychologist, or might harm or exploit the other party.

(b) Likewise, whenever feasible, a psychologist refrains from taking on professional or scientific obligations when preexisting relationships would create a risk of such harm.

(c) If a psychologist finds that, due to unforeseen factors, a potentially harmful multiple relationship has arisen, the psychologist attempts to resolve it with due regard for the best interests of the affected person and maximal compliance with the Ethics Code.

1.18 Barter (With Patients or Clients).

Psychologists ordinarily refrain from accepting goods, services, or other nonmonetary remuneration from patients or clients in return for psychological services because such arrangements create inherent potential for conflicts, exploitation, and distortion of the professional relationship. A psychologist may participate in bartering only if (1) it is not clinically contraindicated, and (2) the relationship is not exploitative. (See also Standards 1.17, Multiple Relationships, and 1.25, Fees and Financial Arrangements.)

1.19 Exploitative Relationships.

(a) Psychologists do not exploit persons over whom they have supervisory, evaluative, or other authority such as students, supervisees, employees, research participants, and clients or patients. (See also Standards 4.05 - 4.07 regarding sexual involvement with clients or patients.)

(b) Psychologists do not engage in sexual relationships with students or supervisees in training over whom the psychologist has evaluative or direct authority, because such relationships are so likely to impair judgment or be exploitative.

1.20 Consultations and Referrals.

(a) Psychologists arrange for appropriate consultations and referrals based principally on the best interests of their patients or clients, with appropriate consent, and subject to other relevant considerations, including applicable law and contractual obligations. (See also Standards 5.01, Discussing the Limits of Confidentiality, and 5.06, Consultations.)

(b) When indicated and professionally appropriate, psychologists cooperate with other professionals in order to serve their patients or clients effectively and appropriately.

(c) Psychologists' referral practices are consistent with law.

1.21 Third-Party Requests for Services.

(a) When a psychologist agrees to provide services to a person or entity at the request of a third party, the psychologist clarifies to the extent feasible, at the outset of the service, the nature of the relationship with each party. This clarification includes the role of the psychologist (such as therapist, organizational consultant, diagnostician, or expert witness), the probable uses of the services provided or the information obtained, and the fact that there may be limits to confidentiality.

(b) If there is a foreseeable risk of the psychologist's being called upon to perform conflicting roles because of the involvement of a third party, the psychologist clarifies the nature and direction of his or her responsibilities, keeps all parties appropriately informed as matters develop, and resolves the situation in accordance with this Ethics Code.

1.22 Delegation to and Supervision of Subordinates.

(a) Psychologists delegate to their employees, supervisees, and research assistants only those responsibilities that such persons can reasonably be expected to perform competently, on the basis of their education, training, or experience, either independently or with the level of supervision being provided.

(b) Psychologists provide proper training and supervision to their employees or supervisees and take reasonable steps to see that such persons perform services responsibly, competently, and ethically.

(c) If institutional policies, procedures, or practices prevent fulfillment of this obligation, psychologists attempt to modify their role or to correct the situation to the extent feasible.

1.23 Documentation of Professional and Scientific Work.

(a) Psychologists appropriately document their professional and scientific work in order to facilitate provision of services later by them or by other professionals, to ensure accountability, and to meet other requirements of institutions or the law.

(b) When psychologists have reason to believe that records of their professional services will be used in legal proceedings involving recipients of or participants in their work, they have a responsibility to create and maintain documentation in the kind of detail and quality that would be consistent with reasonable scrutiny in an adjudicative forum. (See also Standard 7.01, Professionalism, under Forensic Activities.)

1.24 Records and Data.

Psychologists create, maintain, disseminate, store, retain, and dispose of records and data relating to their research, practice, and other work in accordance with law and in a manner that permits compliance with the requirements of this Ethics Code. (See also Standard 5.04, Maintenance of Records.)

1.25 Fees and Financial Arrangements.

(a) As early as is feasible in a professional or scientific relationship, the psychologist and the patient, client, or other appropriate recipient of psychological services reach an agreement specifying the compensation and the billing arrangements.

(b) Psychologists do not exploit recipients of services or payors with respect to fees.

(c) Psychologists' fee practices are consistent with law.

(d) Psychologists do not misrepresent their fees.

(e) If limitations to services can be anticipated because of limitations in financing, this is discussed with the patient, client, or other appropriate recipient of services as early as is feasible. (See also Standard 4.08, Interruption of Services.)

(f) If the patient, client, or other recipient of services does not pay for services as agreed, and if the psychologist wishes to use collection agencies or legal measures to collect the fees, the psychologist first informs the person that such measures will be taken and provides that person an opportunity to make prompt payment. (See also Standard 5.11, Withholding Records for Nonpayment.)

1.26 Accuracy in Reports to Payors and Funding Sources.

In their reports to payors for services or sources of research funding, psychologists accurately state the nature of the research or service provided, the fees or charges, and where applicable, the identity of the provider, the findings, and the diagnosis. (See also Standard 5.05, Disclosures.)

1.27 Referrals and Fees.

When a psychologist pays, receives payment from, or divides fees with another professional other than in an employer - employee relationship, the payment to each is based on the services (clinical, consultative, administrative, or other) provided and is not based on the referral itself.

2. Evaluation, Assessment, or Intervention

2.01 Evaluation, Diagnosis, and Interventions in Professional Context.

(a) Psychologists perform evaluations, diagnostic services, or interventions only within the context of a defined professional relationship. (See also Standards 1.03, Professional and Scientific Relationship.)

(b) Psychologists' assessments, recommendations, reports, and psychological diagnostic or evaluative statements are based on information and techniques (including personal interviews of the individual when appropriate) sufficient to provide appropriate substantiation for their findings. (See also Standard 7.02, Forensic Assessments.)

2.02 Competence and Appropriate Use of Assessments and Interventions.

(a) Psychologists who develop, administer, score, interpret, or use psychological assessment techniques, interviews, tests, or instruments do so in a manner and for purposes that are appropriate in light of the research on or evidence of the usefulness and proper application of the techniques.

(b) Psychologists refrain from misuse of assessment techniques, interventions, results, and interpretations and take reasonable steps to prevent others from misusing the information these techniques provide. This includes refraining from releasing raw test results or raw data to persons, other than to patients or clients as appropriate, who are not qualified to use such information. (See also Standards 1.02, Relationship of Ethics and Law, and 1.04, Boundaries of Competence.)

2.03 Test Construction.

Psychologists who develop and conduct research with tests and other assessment techniques use scientific procedures and current professional knowledge for test design, standardization, validation, reduction or elimination of bias, and recommendations for use.

2.04 Use of Assessment in General and With Special Populations.

(a) Psychologists who perform interventions or administer, score, interpret, or use assessment techniques are familiar with the reliability, validation, and related standardization or outcome studies of, and proper applications and uses of, the techniques they use.

(b) Psychologists recognize limits to the certainty with which diagnoses, judgments, or predictions can be made about individuals.

(c) Psychologists attempt to identify situations in which particular interventions or assessment techniques or norms may not be applicable or may require adjustment in administration or interpretation because of factors such as individuals' gender, age, race, ethnicity, national origin, religion, sexual orientation, disability, language, or socioeconomic status.

2.05 Interpreting Assessment Results.

When interpreting assessment results, including automated interpretations, psychologists take into account the various test factors and characteristics of the person being assessed that might affect psychologists' judgments or reduce the accuracy of their interpretations. They indicate any significant reservations they have about the accuracy or limitations of their interpretations.

2.06 Unqualified Persons.
Psychologists do not promote the use of psychological assessment techniques by unqualified persons. (See also Standard 1.22, Delegation to and Supervision of Subordinates.)

2.07 Obsolete Tests and Outdated Test Results.

(a) Psychologists do not base their assessment or intervention decisions or recommendations on data or test results that are outdated for the current purpose.

(b) Similarly, psychologists do not base such decisions or recommendations on tests and measures that are obsolete and not useful for the current purpose.

2.08 Test Scoring and Interpretation Services.

(a) Psychologists who offer assessment or scoring procedures to other professionals accurately describe the purpose, norms, validity, reliability, and applications of the procedures and any special qualifications applicable to their use.

(b) Psychologists select scoring and interpretation services (including automated services) on the basis of evidence of the validity of the program and procedures as well as on other appropriate considerations.

(c) Psychologists retain appropriate responsibility for the appropriate application, interpretation, and use of assessment instruments, whether they score and interpret such tests themselves or use automated or other services.

2.09 Explaining Assessment Results.
Unless the nature of the relationship is clearly explained to the person being assessed in advance and precludes provision of an explanation of results (such as in some organizational consulting, pre-employment or security screenings, and forensic evaluations), psychologists ensure that an explanation of the results is provided using language that is reasonably understandable to the person assessed or to another legally authorized person on behalf of the client. Regardless of whether the scoring and interpretation are done by the psychologist, by

assistants, or by automated or other outside services, psychologists take reasonable steps to ensure that appropriate explanations of results are given.

2.10 Maintaining Test Security.
Psychologists make reasonable efforts to maintain the integrity and security of tests and other assessment techniques consistent with law, contractual obligations, and in a manner that permits compliance with the requirements of this Ethics Code. (See also Standard 1.02, Relationship of Ethics and Law.)

3. Advertising and Other Public Statements

3.01 Definition of Public Statements.
Psychologists comply with this Ethics Code in public statements relating to their professional services, products, or publications or to the field of psychology. Public statements include but are not limited to paid or unpaid advertising, brochures, printed matter, directory listings, personal resumes or curriculum vitae, interviews or comments for use in media, statements in legal proceedings, lectures and public oral presentations, and published materials.

3.02 Statements by Others.

(a) Psychologists who engage others to create or place public statements that promote their professional practice, products, or activities retain professional responsibility for such statements.

(b) In addition, psychologists make reasonable efforts to prevent others whom they do not control (such as employers, publishers, sponsors, organizational clients, and representatives of the print or broadcast media) from making deceptive statements concerning psychologists' practice or professional or scientific activities.

(c) If psychologists learn of deceptive statements about their work made by others, psychologists make reasonable efforts to correct such statements.

(d) Psychologists do not compensate employees of press, radio, television, or other communication media in return for publicity in a news item.

(e) A paid advertisement relating to the psychologist's activities must be identified as such, unless it is already apparent from the context.

3.03 Avoidance of False or Deceptive Statements.

(a) Psychologists do not make public statements that are false, deceptive, misleading, or fraudulent, either because of what they state, convey, or suggest or because of what they omit, concerning their research, practice, or other work activities or those of per- sons or organizations with which they are affiliated. As examples (and not in limitation) of this standard, psychologists do not make false or deceptive statements concerning (1) their training, experience, or competence; (2) their academic degrees; (3) their credentials; (4) their institutional or association affiliations; (5) their services; (6) the scientific or clinical basis for, or results or degree of success of, their services; (7) their fees; or (8) their publications or research findings. (See also Standards 6.15, Deception in Research, and 6.18, Providing Participants With Information About the Study.)

(b) Psychologists claim as credentials for their psychological work, only degrees that (1) were earned from a regionally accredited educational institution or (2) were the basis for psychology licensure by the state in which they practice.

3.04 Media Presentations.

When psychologists provide advice or comment by means of public lectures, demonstrations, radio or television programs, prerecorded tapes, printed articles, mailed material, or other media, they take reasonable precautions to ensure that (1) the statements are based on appropriate psychological literature and practice, (2) the statements are otherwise consistent with this Ethics Code, and (3) the recipients of the information are not encouraged to infer that a relationship has been established with them personally.

3.05 Testimonials.

Psychologists do not solicit testimonials from current psychotherapy clients or patients or other persons who because of their particular circumstances are vulnerable to undue influence.

3.06 In-Person Solicitation.

Psychologists do not engage, directly or through agents, in uninvited in-person solicitation of business from actual or potential psychotherapy patients or clients or other persons who because of their particular circumstances are vulnerable to undue influence. However, this does not preclude attempting to implement appropriate collateral contacts with significant others for the purpose of benefiting an already engaged therapy patient.

4. Therapy

4.01 Structuring the Relationship.

(a) Psychologists discuss with clients or patients as early as is feasible in the therapeutic relationship appropriate issues, such as the nature and anticipated course of therapy, fees, and confidentiality. (See also Standards 1.25, Fees and Financial Arrangements, and 5.01, Discussing the Limits of Confidentiality.)

(b) When the psychologist's work with clients or patients will be supervised, the above discussion includes that fact, and the name of the supervisor, when the supervisor has legal responsibility for the case.

(c) When the therapist is a student intern, the client or patient is informed of that fact.

(d) Psychologists make reasonable efforts to answer patients' questions and to avoid apparent misunderstandings about therapy. Whenever possible, psychologists provide oral and/or written information, using language that is reasonably understandable to the patient or client.

4.02 Informed Consent to Therapy.

(a) Psychologists obtain appropriate informed consent to therapy or related procedures, using language that is reasonably understandable to participants. The content of informed consent will vary depending on many circumstances; however, informed consent generally implies that the person (1) has the capacity to consent, (2) has been informed of significant information concerning the procedure, (3) has freely and without undue influence expressed consent, and (4) consent has been appropriately documented.

(b) When persons are legally incapable of giving informed consent, psychologists obtain informed permission from a legally authorized person, if such substitute consent is permitted by law.

(c) In addition, psychologists (1) inform those persons who

are legally incapable of giving informed consent about the proposed interventions in a manner commensurate with the persons' psychological capacities, (2) seek their assent to those interventions, and (3) consider such persons' preferences and best interests.

4.03 Couple and Family Relationships.

(a) When a psychologist agrees to provide services to several persons who have a relationship (such as husband and wife or parents and children), the psychologist attempts to clarify at the outset (1) which of the individuals are patients or clients and (2) the relationship the psychologist will have with each person. This clarification includes the role of the psychologist and the probable uses of the services provided or the information obtained. (See also Standard 5.01, Discussing the Limits of Confidentiality.)

(b) As soon as it becomes apparent that the psychologist may be called on to perform potentially conflicting roles (such as marital counselor to husband and wife, and then witness for one party in a divorce proceeding), the psychologist attempts to clarify and adjust, or withdraw from, roles appropriately. (See also Standard 7.03, Clarification of Role, under Forensic Activities.)

4.04 Providing Mental Health Services to Those Served by Others.

In deciding whether to offer or provide services to those already receiving mental health services elsewhere, psychologists carefully consider the treatment issues and the potential patient's or client's welfare. The psychologist discusses these issues with the patient or client, or another legally authorized person on behalf of the client, in order to minimize the risk of confusion and conflict, consults with the other service providers when appropriate, and proceeds with caution and sensitivity to the therapeutic issues.

4.05 Sexual Intimacies With Current Patients or Clients.

Psychologists do not engage in sexual intimacies with current patients or clients.

4.06 Therapy With Former Sexual Partners.

Psychologists do not accept as therapy patients or clients persons with whom they have engaged in sexual intimacies.

4.07 Sexual Intimacies With Former Therapy Patients.

(a) Psychologists do not engage in sexual intimacies with a former therapy patient or client for at least two years after cessation or termination of professional services.

(b) Because sexual intimacies with a former therapy patient or client are so frequently harmful to the patient or client, and because such intimacies undermine public confidence in the psychology profession and thereby deter the public's use of needed services, psychologists do not engage in sexual intimacies with former therapy patients and clients even after a two-year interval except in the most unusual circumstances. The psychologist who engages in such activity after the two years following cessation or termination of treatment bears the burden of demonstrating that there has been no exploitation, in light of all relevant factors, including (1) the amount of time that has passed since therapy terminated, (2) the nature and duration of the therapy, (3) the circumstances of termination, (4) the patient's or client's personal history, (5) the patient's or client's current mental status, (6) the likelihood of adverse impact on the patient or client and others, and (7) any statements or actions made by the therapist during the course of therapy suggesting or inviting the possibility of a post-termination sexual or romantic relationship with the patient or client. (See also Standard 1.17, Multiple Relationships.)

4.08 Interruption of Services.

(a) Psychologists make reasonable efforts to plan for facilitating care in the event that psychological services are interrupted by factors such as the psychologist's illness, death, unavailability, or relocation or by the client's relocation or financial limitations. (See also Standard 5.09, Preserving Records and Data.)

(b) When entering into employment or contractual relationships, psychologists provide for orderly and appropriate resolution of responsibility for patient or client care in the event that the employment or contractual relationship ends, with paramount consideration given to the welfare of the patient or client.

4.09 Terminating the Professional Relationship.

(a) Psychologists do not abandon patients or clients. (See also Standard 1.25e, under Fees and Financial Arrangements.)

(b) Psychologists terminate a professional relationship when it becomes reasonably clear that the patient or client no longer needs the service, is not benefiting, or is being harmed by continued service.

(c) Prior to termination for whatever reason, except where precluded by the patient's or client's conduct, the psychologist discusses the patient's or client's views and needs, provides appropriate pretermination counseling, suggests alternative service providers as appropriate, and takes other reasonable steps to facilitate transfer of responsibility to another provider if the patient or client needs one immediately.

5.Privacy and Condifentiqality

These Standards are potentially applicable to the professional and scientific activities of all psychologists.

5.01 Discussing the Limits of Confidentiality.

(a) Psychologists discuss with persons and organizations with whom they establish a scientific or professional relationship (including, to the extent feasible, minors and their legal representatives) (1) the relevant limitations on confidentiality, including limitations where applicable in group, marital, and family therapy or in organizational consulting, and (2) the foreseeable uses of the information generated through their services.

(b) Unless it is not feasible or is contraindicated, the discussion of confidentiality occurs at the outset of the relationship and thereafter as new circumstances may warrant.

(c) Permission for electronic recording of interviews is secured from clients and patients.

5.02 Maintaining Confidentiality.

Psychologists have a primary obligation and take reasonable precautions to respect the confidentiality rights of those with whom they work or consult, recognizing that confidentiality may be established by law, institutional rules, or professional or scientific relationships. (See also Standard 6.26, Professional Reviewers.)

5.03 Minimizing Intrusions on Privacy.

(a) In order to minimize intrusions on privacy, psychologists include in written and oral reports, consultations, and the like, only information germane to the purpose for which the communication is made.

(b) Psychologists discuss confidential information obtained in clinical or consulting relationships, or evaluative data concerning patients, individual or organizational clients, students, research participants, supervisees, and employees, only for appropriate scientific or professional purposes and only with persons clearly concerned with such matters.

5.04 Maintenance of Records.
Psychologists maintain appropriate confidentiality in creating, storing, accessing, transferring, and disposing of records under their control, whether these are written, automated, or in any other medium. Psychologists maintain and dispose of records in accordance with law and in a manner that permits compliance with the requirements of this Ethics Code.

5.05 Disclosures.

(a) Psychologists disclose confidential information without the consent of the individual only as mandated by law, or where permitted by law for a valid purpose, such as (1) to provide needed professional services to the patient or the individual or organizational client, (2) to obtain appropriate professional consultations, (3) to protect the patient or client or others from harm, or (4) to obtain payment for services, in which instance disclosure is limited to the minimum that is necessary to achieve the purpose.

(b) Psychologists also may disclose confidential information with the appropriate consent of the patient or the individual or organizational client (or of another legally authorized person on behalf of the patient or client), unless prohibited by law.

5.06 Consultations.
When consulting with colleagues, (1) psychologists do not share confidential information that reasonably could lead to the identification of a patient, client, research participant, or other person or organization with whom they have a confidential relationship unless they have obtained the prior consent of the person or organization or the disclosure cannot be avoided, and (2) they share information only to the extent necessary to

achieve the purposes of the consultation. (See also Standard 5.02, Maintaining Confidentiality.)

5.07 Confidential Information in Databases.

(a) If confidential information concerning recipients of psychological services is to be entered into databases or systems of records available to persons whose access has not been consented to by the recipient, then psychologists use coding or other techniques to avoid the inclusion of personal identifiers.

(b) If a research protocol approved by an institutional review board or similar body requires the inclusion of personal identifiers, such identifiers are deleted before the information is made accessible to persons other than those of whom the subject was advised.

(c) If such deletion is not feasible, then before psychologists transfer such data to others or review such data collected by others, they take reasonable steps to determine that appropriate consent of personally identifiable individuals has been obtained.

5.08 Use of Confidential Information for Didactic or Other Purposes.

(a) Psychologists do not disclose in their writings, lectures, or other public media, confidential, personally identifiable information concerning their patients, individual or organizational clients, students, research participants, or other recipients of their services that they obtained during the course of their work, unless the person or organization has consented in writing or unless there is other ethical or legal authorization for doing so.

(b) Ordinarily, in such scientific and professional presentations, psychologists disguise confidential information concerning such persons or organizations so that they are not individually identifiable to others and so that discussions do not cause harm to subjects who might identify themselves.

5.09 Preserving Records and Data.

A psychologist makes plans in advance so that confidentiality of records and data is protected in the event of the psychologist's death, incapacity, or withdrawal from the position or practice.

5.10 Ownership of Records and Data.
Recognizing that ownership of records and data is governed by legal principles, psychologists take reasonable and lawful steps so that records and data remain available to the extent needed to serve the best interests of patients, individual or organizational clients, research participants, or appropriate others.

5.11 Withholding Records for Nonpayment.
Psychologists may not withhold records under their control that are requested and imminently needed for a patient's or client's treatment solely because payment has not been received, except as otherwise provided by law.

6. Teaching, Training, Supervision, Research, and Publishing
6.01 Design of Education and Training Programs.
Psychologists who are responsible for education and training programs seek to ensure that the programs are competently designed, provide the proper experiences, and meet the requirements for licensure, certification, or other goals for which claims are made by the program.

6.02 Descriptions of Education and Training Programs.
(a) Psychologists responsible for education and training programs seek to ensure that there is a current and accurate description of the program content, training goals and objectives, and requirements that must be met for satisfactory completion of the program. This information must be made readily available to all interested parties.
(b) Psychologists seek to ensure that statements concerning their course outlines are accurate and not misleading, particularly regarding the subject matter to be covered, bases for evaluating progress, and the nature of course experiences. (See also Standard 3.03, Avoidance of False or Deceptive Statements.)
(c) To the degree to which they exercise control, psychologists responsible for announcements, catalogs, brochures, or advertisements describing workshops, seminars, or other non-degree- granting educational programs ensure that they accurately describe the audience for which the program is intended, the educational objectives, the presenters, and the fees in-

volved.

6.03 Accuracy and Objectivity in Teaching.

(a) When engaged in teaching or training, psychologists present psychological information accurately and with a reasonable degree of objectivity.

(b) When engaged in teaching or training, psychologists recognize the power they hold over students or supervisees and therefore make reasonable efforts to avoid engaging in conduct that is personally demeaning to students or supervisees. (See also Standards 1.09, Respecting Others, and 1.12, Other Harassment.)

6.04 Limitation on Teaching.

Psychologists do not teach the use of techniques or procedures that require specialized training, licensure, or expertise, including but not limited to hypnosis, biofeedback, and projective techniques, to individuals who lack the prerequisite training, legal scope of practice, or expertise.

6.05 Assessing Student and Supervisee Performance.

(a) In academic and supervisory relationships, psychologists establish an appropriate process for providing feedback to students and supervisees.

(b) Psychologists evaluate students and supervisees on the basis of their actual performance on relevant and established program requirements.

6.06 Planning Research.

(a) Psychologists design, conduct, and report research in accordance with recognized standards of scientific competence and ethical research.

(b) Psychologists plan their research so as to minimize the possibility that results will be misleading.

(c) In planning research, psychologists consider its ethical acceptability under the Ethics Code. If an ethical issue is unclear, psychologists seek to resolve the issue through consultation with institutional review boards, animal care and use committees, peer consultations, or other proper mechanisms.

(d) Psychologists take reasonable steps to implement appropriate protections for the rights and welfare of human participants, other persons affected by the research, and the welfare of animal subjects.

6.07 Responsibility.

(a) Psychologists conduct research competently and with due concern for the dignity and welfare of the participants.

(b) Psychologists are responsible for the ethical conduct of research conducted by them or by others under their supervision or control.

(c) Researchers and assistants are permitted to perform only those tasks for which they are appropriately trained and prepared.

(d) As part of the process of development and implementation of research projects, psychologists consult those with expertise concerning any special population under investigation or most likely to be affected.

6.08 Compliance With Law and Standards.
Psychologists plan and conduct research in a manner consistent with federal and state law and regulations, as well as professional standards governing the conduct of research, and particularly those standards governing research with human participants and animal subjects.

6.09 Institutional Approval.
Psychologists obtain from host institutions or organizations appropriate approval prior to conducting research, and they provide accurate information about their research proposals. They conduct the research in accordance with the approved research protocol.

6.10 Research Responsibilities.
Prior to conducting research (except research involving only anonymous surveys, naturalistic observations, or similar research), psychologists enter into an agreement with participants that clarifies the nature of the research and the responsibilities of each party.

6.11 Informed Consent to Research.

(a) Psychologists use language that is reasonably understandable to research participants in obtaining their appropriate informed consent (except as provided in Standard 6.12, Dispensing with Informed Consent). Such informed consent is appropriately documented.

(b) Using language that is reasonably understandable to participants, psychologists inform participants of the nature of the research; they inform participants that they are free to participate or to decline to participate or to withdraw from the research; they explain the foreseeable consequences of declining or withdrawing; they inform participants of significant factors that may be expected to influence their willingness to participate (such as risks, discomfort, adverse effects, or limitations on confidentiality, except as provided in Standard 6.15, Deception in Research); and they explain other aspects about which the prospective participants inquire.

(c) When psychologists conduct research with individuals such as students or subordinates, psychologists take special care to protect the prospective participants from adverse consequences of declining or withdrawing from participation.

(d) When research participation is a course requirement or opportunity for extra credit, the prospective participant is given the choice of equitable alternative activities.

(e) For persons who are legally incapable of giving informed consent, psychologists nevertheless (1) provide an appropriate explanation, (2) obtain the participant's assent, and (3) obtain appropriate permission from a legally authorized person, if such substitute consent is permitted by law.

6.12 Dispensing With Informed Consent.

Before determining that planned research (such as research involving only anonymous questionnaires, naturalistic observations, or certain kinds of archival research) does not require the informed consent of research participants, psychologists consider applicable regulations and institutional review board requirements, and they consult with colleagues as appropriate.

6.13 Informed Consent in Research Filming or Recording.

Psychologists obtain informed consent from research participants prior to filming or recording them in any form, unless the research involves simply naturalistic observations in public places and it is not anticipated that the recording will be used in a manner that could cause personal identification or harm.

6.14 Offering Inducements for Research Participants.

(a) In offering professional services as an inducement to obtain research participants, psychologists make clear the nature of the services, as well as the risks, obligations, and limitations. (See also Standard 1.18, Barter [With Patients or Clients].)

(b) Psychologists do not offer excessive or inappropriate financial or other inducements to obtain research participants, particularly when it might tend to coerce participation.

6.15 Deception in Research.

(a) Psychologists do not conduct a study involving deception unless they have determined that the use of deceptive techniques is justified by the study's prospective scientific, educational, or applied value and that equally effective alternative procedures that do not use deception are not feasible.

(b) Psychologists never deceive research participants about significant aspects that would affect their willingness to participate, such as physical risks, discomfort, or unpleasant emotional experiences.

(c) Any other deception that is an integral feature of the design and conduct of an experiment must be explained to participants as early as is feasible, preferably at the conclusion of their participation, but no later than at the conclusion of the research. (See also Standard 6.18, Providing Participants With Information About the Study.)

6.16 Sharing and Utilizing Data.

Psychologists inform research participants of their anticipated sharing or further use of personally identifiable research data and of the possibility of unanticipated future uses.

6.17 Minimizing Invasiveness.

In conducting research, psychologists interfere with the participants or milieu from which data are collected only in a manner that is warranted by an appropriate research design and that is consistent with psychologists' roles as scientific investigators.

6.18 Providing Participants With Information About the Study.

(a) Psychologists provide a prompt opportunity for participants to obtain appropriate information about the nature, results, and conclusions of the research, and psychologists attempt to correct any misconceptions that participants may have.

(b) If scientific or humane values justify delaying or withholding this information, psychologists take reasonable measures to reduce the risk of harm.

6.19 Honoring Commitments.
Psychologists take reasonable measures to honor all commitments they have made to research participants.

6.20 Care and Use of Animals in Research.

(a) Psychologists who conduct research involving animals treat them humanely.

(b) Psychologists acquire, care for, use, and dispose of animals in compliance with current federal, state, and local laws and regulations, and with professional standards.

(c) Psychologists trained in research methods and experienced in the care of laboratory animals supervise all procedures involving animals and are responsible for ensuring appropriate consideration of their comfort, health, and humane treatment.

(d) Psychologists ensure that all individuals using animals under their supervision have received instruction in research methods and in the care, maintenance, and handling of the species being used, to the extent appropriate to their role.

(e) Responsibilities and activities of individuals assisting in a research project are consistent with their respective competencies.

(f) Psychologists make reasonable efforts to minimize the discomfort, infection, illness, and pain of animal subjects.

(g) A procedure subjecting animals to pain, stress, or privation is used only when an alternative procedure is unavailable and the goal is justified by its prospective scientific, educational, or applied value.

(h) Surgical procedures are performed under appropriate anesthesia; techniques to avoid infection and minimize pain are followed during and after surgery.

(i) When it is appropriate that the animal's life be terminated, it is done rapidly, with an effort to minimize pain, and in accordance with accepted procedures.

6.21 Reporting of Results.

(a) Psychologists do not fabricate data or falsify results in their publications.

(b) If psychologists discover significant errors in their published data, they take reasonable steps to correct such errors in a correction, retraction, erratum, or other appropriate publication means.

6.22 Plagiarism.

Psychologists do not present substantial portions or elements of another's work or data as their own, even if the other work or data source is cited occasionally.

6.23 Publication Credit.

(a) Psychologists take responsibility and credit, including authorship credit, only for work they have actually performed or to which they have contributed.

(b) Principal authorship and other publication credits accurately reflect the relative scientific or professional contributions of the individuals involved, regardless of their relative status. Mere possession of an institutional position, such as Department Chair, does not justify authorship credit. Minor contributions to the research or to the writing for publications are appropriately acknowledged, such as in footnotes or in an introductory statement.

(c) A student is usually listed as principal author on any multiple-authored article that is substantially based on the student's dissertation or thesis.

6.24 Duplicate Publication of Data.

Psychologists do not publish, as original data, data that have been previously published. This does not preclude republishing data when they are accompanied by proper acknowledgment.

6.25 Sharing Data.

After research results are published, psychologists do not withhold the data on which their conclusions are based from other competent professionals who seek to verify the substantive claims through reanalysis and who intend to use such data only for that purpose, provided that the confidentiality of the participants can be protected and unless legal rights concerning proprietary data preclude their release.

6.26 Professional Reviewers.
Psychologists who review material submitted for publication, grant, or other research proposal review respect the confidentiality of and the proprietary rights in such information of those who submitted it.

7. FORENSIC ACTIVITIES

7.01 Professionalism.
Psychologists who perform forensic functions, such as assessments, interviews, consultations, reports, or expert testimony, must comply with all other provisions of this Ethics Code to the extent that they apply to such activities. In addition, psychologists base their forensic work on appropriate knowledge of and competence in the areas underlying such work, including specialized knowledge concerning special populations. (See also Standards 1.06, Basis for Scientific and Professional Judgments; 1.08, Human Differences; 1.15, Misuse of Psychologists' Influence; and 1.23, Documentation of Professional and Scientific Work.)

7.02 Forensic Assessments.

(a) Psychologists' forensic assessments, recommendations, and reports are based on information and techniques (including personal interviews of the individual, when appropriate) sufficient to provide appropriate substantiation for their findings. (See also Standards 1.03, Professional and Scientific Relationship; 1.23, Documentation of Professional and Scientific Work; 2.01, Evaluation, Diagnosis, and Interventions in Professional Context; and 2.05, Interpreting Assessment Results.)

(b) Except as noted in (c), below, psychologists provide written or oral forensic reports or testimony of the psychological characteristics of an individual only after they have conducted an examination of the individual adequate to support their statements or conclusions.

(c) When, despite reasonable efforts, such an examination is not feasible, psychologists clarify the impact of their limited information on the reliability and validity of their reports and testimony, and they appropriately limit the nature and extent of their conclusions or recommendations.

7.03 Clarification of Role.
In most circumstances, psychologists avoid performing multiple and potentially conflicting roles in forensic matters. When psychologists may be called on to serve in more than one role in a legal proceeding - for example, as consultant or expert for one party or for the court and as a fact witness - they clarify role expectations and the extent of confidentiality in advance to the extent feasible, and thereafter as changes occur, in order to avoid compromising their professional judgment and objectivity and in order to avoid misleading others regarding their role.

7.04 Truthfulness and Candor.
(a) In forensic testimony and reports, psychologists testify truthfully, honestly, and candidly and, consistent with applicable legal procedures, describe fairly the bases for their testimony and conclusions.
(b) Whenever necessary to avoid misleading, psychologists acknowledge the limits of their data or conclusions.

7.05 Prior Relationships.
A prior professional relationship with a party does not preclude psychologists from testifying as fact witnesses or from testifying to their services to the extent permitted by applicable law. Psychologists appropriately take into account ways in which the prior relationship might affect their professional objectivity or opinions and disclose the potential conflict to the relevant par- ties.

7.06 Compliance With Law and Rules.
In performing forensic roles, psychologists are reasonably familiar with the rules governing their roles. Psychologists are aware of the occasionally competing demands placed upon them by these principles and the requirements of the court system, and attempt to resolve these conflicts by making known their commitment to this Ethics Code and taking steps to resolve the conflict in a responsible manner. (See also Standard 1.02, Relationship of Ethics and Law.)

8. RESOLVING ETHICAL ISSUES

8.01 Familiarity With Ethics Code.
Psychologists have an obligation to be familiar with this Ethics Code, other applicable ethics codes, and their application to psychologists' work. Lack of awareness or misunderstanding of an ethical standard is not itself a defense to a charge of unethical conduct.

8.02 Confronting Ethical Issues.
When a psychologist is uncertain whether a particular situation or course of action would violate this Ethics Code, the psychologist ordinarily consults with other psychologists knowledgeable about ethical issues, with state or national psychology ethics committees, or with other appropriate authorities in order to choose a proper response.

8.03 Conflicts Between Ethics and Organizational Demands.
If the demands of an organization with which psychologists are affiliated conflict with this Ethics Code, psychologists clarify the nature of the conflict, make known their commitment to the Ethics Code, and to the extent feasible, seek to resolve the conflict in a way that permits the fullest adherence to the Ethics Code.

8.04 Informal Resolution of Ethical Violations.
When psychologists believe that there may have been an ethical violation by another psychologist, they attempt to resolve the issue by bringing it to the attention of that individual if an informal resolution appears appropriate and the intervention does not violate any confidentiality rights that may be involved.

8.05 Reporting Ethical Violations.
If an apparent ethical violation is not appropriate for informal resolution under Standard 8.04 or is not resolved properly in that fashion, psychologists take further action appropriate to the situation, unless such action conflicts with confidentiality rights in ways that cannot be resolved. Such action might include referral to state or national committees on professional ethics or to state licensing boards.

8.06 Cooperating With Ethics Committees.
Psychologists cooperate in ethics investigations, proceedings,

and resulting requirements of the APA or any affiliated state psychological association to which they belong. In doing so, they make reasonable efforts to resolve any issues as to confidentiality. Failure to cooperate is itself an ethics violation.

8.07 Improper Complaints.
Psychologists do not file or encourage the filing of ethics complaints that are frivolous and are intended to harm the respondent rather than to protect the public.

History and effective date.
This version of the APA Ethics Code was adopted by the American Psychological Association's Council of Representatives during its meeting, August 13 and 16, 1992, and is effective beginning December 1, 1992. Inquiries concerning the substance or interpretation of the APA Ethics Code should be addressed to the Director, Office of Ethics, American Psychological Association, 750 First Street, NE, Washington, DC 20002-4242.

This Code will be used to adjudicate complaints brought concerning alleged conduct occurring after the effective date. Complaints regarding conduct occurring prior to the effective date will be adjudicated on the basis of the version of the Code that was in effect at the time the conduct occurred, except that no provisions repealed in June 1989, will be enforced even if an earlier version contains the provision. The Ethics Code will undergo continuing review and study for future revisions; comments on the Code may be sent to the above address.

The APA has previously published its Ethical Standards as follows:

American Psychological Association. (1953). Ethical standards of psychologists. Washington, DC: Author.

American Psychological Association. (1958). Standards of ethical behavior for psychologists. American Psychologist, 13, 268- 271.

American Psychological Association. (1963). Ethical standards of psychologists. American Psychologist, 18, 56-60.

American Psychological Association. (1968). Ethical standards of psychologists. American Psychologist, 23, 357-361.

American Psychological Association. (1977, March). Ethical standards of psychologists. APA Monitor, 22-23.

American Psychological Association. (1979). Ethical

standards of psychologists. Washington, DC: Author.
American Psychological Association. (1981). Ethical principles of psychologists. American Psychologist, 36, 633-638.
American Psychological Association. (1990). Ethical principles of psychologists (Amended June 2, 1989). American Psychologist, 45, 390-395.

Request copies of the APA's Ethical Principles of Psychologists and Code of Conduct from the APA Order Department, 750 First Street, NE, Washington, DC 20002-4242, or phone (202) 336-5510.

Footnote 1:
Professional materials that are most helpful in this regard are guidelines and standards that have been adopted or endorsed by professional psychological organizations. Such guidelines and standards, whether adopted by the American Psychological Association (APA) or its Divisions, are not enforceable as such by this Ethics Code, but are of educative value to psychologists, courts, and professional bodies. Such materials include, but are not limited to, the APA's General Guidelines for Providers of Psychological Services (1987), Specialty Guidelines for the Delivery of Services by Clinical Psychologists, Counseling Psychologists, Industrial/Organizational Psychologists, and School Psychologists (1981), Guidelines for Computer Based Tests and Interpretations (1987), Standards for Educational and Psychological Testing (1985), Ethical Principles in the Conduct of Research With Human Participants (1982), Guidelines for Ethical Conduct in the Care and Use of Animals (1986), Guidelines for Providers of Psychological Services to Ethnic, Linguistic, and Culturally Diverse Populations (1990), and Publication Manual of the American Psychological Association (3rd ed., 1983). Materials not adopted by APA as a whole include the APA Division 41 (Forensic Psychology)/American Psychology-Law Society's Specialty Guidelines for Forensic Psychologists (1991).

APPENDIX C

Ethical Standards for Marriage and Family Therapists

PART I - STANDARDS

1. RESPONSIBILITY TO PATIENTS[1]
2. CONFIDENTIALITY
3. PROFESSIONAL COMPETENCE AND INTEGRITY
4. RESPONSIBILITY TO STUDENTS AND SUPERVISEES
4. RESPONSIBILITY TO COLLEAGUES
6. RESPONSIBILITY TO RESEARCH PARTICIPANTS
7. RESPONSIBILITY TO THE PROFESSION
8. RESPONSIBILITY TO THE LEGAL SYSTEM
9. FINANCIAL ARRANGEMENTS
10. ADVERTISING

The Board of Directors of CAMFT hereby promulgates, pursuant to Article VI, Section A 1. and 2. and Article VII, Section B 3. of the Association Bylaws, a Revised Code of Ethical Standards for Marriage and Family Therapists. Members of CAMFT are expected to be familiar with and abide by these standards and by applicable California laws and regulations governing the conduct of licensed marriage, family and child counselors, interns and trainees. The effective date of these revised standards is June 7, 1997.

The practice of marriage, family and child counseling and psychotherapy[i] is both an art and a science. It is varied and often complex. These ethical standards are to be read, understood, and utilized as a guide for ethical behavior. The general principles contained in this code of conduct are also used as a basis for the adjudication of ethical issues and/or complaints (both within and outside of CAMFT) which may arise. Ethical behavior, in a given situation, must satisfy not only the judgment of the individual marriage, family and child therapist, but also the judgment of his/her peers, based upon a set of recognized norms.

We recognize that the development of standards is an ongoing process, and that every conceivable situation that may occur cannot be expressly covered by any set of standards. The absence of a specific prohibition against a particular kind of conduct does not mean that such conduct is either ethical or unethical. While the specific wording of these standards is important, the spirit and intent of the principles should always be taken into consideration by those utilizing or interpreting this code.

Violations of these standards should be brought to the attention of the CAMFT Ethics Committee, in writing, at CAMFT's administrative office, 7901 Raytheon Road, San Diego, CA 92111-1606, or at such other address as may be necessary because of a change in location of the administrative office.

1. RESPONSIBILITY TO PATIENTS[ii]

Marriage and family therapists[iii] advance the welfare of families and individuals, respect the rights of those persons seeking their assistance, and make reasonable efforts to ensure that their services are used appropriately.

1.1 Marriage and family therapists do not condone, engage in discrimination, or refuse professional service to anyone on the basis of race, gender, religion, national origin, age, sexual orientation, disability, socioeconomic or marital status. Marriage and family therapists make reasonable efforts to accommodate patients who have physical disabilities.

1.2 Marriage and family therapists are aware of their influential position with respect to patients, and they avoid exploiting the trust and dependency of such persons. Marriage and family therapists therefore avoid dual relationships[iv] with patients that are reasonably likely to impair professional judgment or lead to exploitation. A dual relationship occurs when a therapist and his/her patient engage in a separate and distinct relationship either simultaneously with the therapeutic relationship, or during a reasonable period of time following the termination of the therapeutic relationship. Not all dual relationships are unethical, and some dual relationships cannot be avoided. When a dual relationship cannot be avoided, therapists take appropriate professional precautions to insure that judgment is not impaired and that no exploitation occurs.

1.2.1 Sexual intercourse, sexual contact or sexual intimacy with a patient, or a patient's spouse or partner, during the therapeutic relationship, or during the two years following the termination of the therapeutic relationship, is unethical.

1.2.2 Other acts which would result in unethical dual relationships include, but are not limited to, borrowing money from a patient, hiring a patient, engaging in a business venture with a patient, or engaging in a close personal relationship with a patient.

1.3 Marriage and family therapists do not enter into therapeutic relationships with persons with whom they have had a sexual relationship.

1.4 Marriage and family therapists are encouraged to inform patients of the potential risks and benefits of services.

1.5 Marriage and family therapists do not use their professional relationships with patients to further their own interests.

1.6 Marriage and family therapists continue therapeutic relationships only so long as it is reasonably clear that patients are benefiting from the relationship. It is unethical to maintain a professional or therapeutic relationship for the sole purpose of financial gain to the therapist.

1.7 Marriage and family therapists respect the right of patients to make decisions and help them to understand the consequences of these decisions. Marriage and family therapists advise their patients that decisions on the status of relationships are the responsibilities of the patient(s).

1.8 Marriage and family therapists inform patients of the extent of their availability for emergencies and for other contacts between sessions.

1.9 Marriage and family therapists assist persons in obtaining other therapeutic services if a therapist is unable or unwilling to provide professional help.

1.10 Marriage and family therapists do not abandon or neglect patients in treatment. If a therapist is unable to continue to provide care, the therapist will assist the patient in making reasonable arrangements for continuation of treatment.

1.11 When terminating employment or contractual relationships, marriage and family therapists primarily consider the best interests of the patient when resolving issues of continued responsibility for patient care.

1.12 Marriage and family therapists, when treating a family unit(s), shall carefully consider the potential conflict that may arise between the family unit(s) and each individual. Marriage and family therapists clarify at the commencement of therapy which person or persons are clients and the nature of the relationship(s) the therapist will have with each person involved in the treatment.

1.13 Marriage and family therapists obtain written informed consent from clients before video taping, audio recording, or permitting third party observation.

1.14 Marriage and family therapists do not withhold patient records or information solely because the therapist has not been paid for prior therapy services.

1.15Marriage and family therapists consult, associate, collaborate with, and refer to physicians, other health care professionals, and community resources in order to improve and protect the health and welfare of the patient.

1.16 Marriage and family therapists advocate for mental health care they believe will benefit their patients. In appropriate circumstances, they challenge denials of care, or denials of payment for care, by managed care organizations, insurers, or other payers.

1.17 Marriage and family therapists disclose treatment alternatives to patients, whether or not there is coverage for such treatment under the terms of a managed care plan, insurance policy, or other health care plan.

2. CONFIDENTIALITY

Marriage and family therapists have unique confidentiality responsibilities because the "patient" in a therapeutic relationship may be more than one person. The overriding principle is that marriage and family therapists respect the confidences of their patient(s).

2.1 Marriage and family therapists do not disclose patient confidences, including the names or identities of their patients, to anyone except a) as mandated by law b) as permitted by law c) when the marriage and family therapist is a defendant in a civil, criminal or disciplinary action arising from the therapy (in which case patient confidences may only be disclosed in the course of that action), or d) if there is an authorization previously obtained in writing, and then such information may only be revealed in accordance with the terms of the authorization.

2.2 In circumstances when more than one person in a family is receiving therapy or treatment, and when a third party seeks information related to any aspect of such treatment, each family member receiving therapy or treatment who is legally competent to execute an authorization must sign the authorization before a marriage and family therapist will disclose information received from any family member.

2.3 Marriage and family therapists are aware of the possible adverse effects of technological changes with respect to the dissemination of patient information, and take reasonable care when disclosing such information.

2.4 Marriage and family therapists store, transfer, and/or dispose of patient records in ways that protect confidentiality.

2.5 Marriage and family therapists take appropriate steps to ensure, insofar as possible, that the confidentiality of patients is maintained by their employees, supervisees, assistants and volunteers.

2.6 Marriage and family therapists use clinical materials in teaching, writing, and public presentations only if a written authorization has been previously obtained in accordance with 2.1 d, or when appropriate steps have been taken to protect patient identity.

2.7 Marriage and family therapists, when working with a group, explain to the group the importance of maintaining confidentiality, and are encouraged to obtain agreement from group participants to respect the confidentiality of other members of the group.

3. PROFESSIONAL COMPETENCE AND INTEGRITY

Marriage and family therapists maintain high standards of professional competence and integrity.

3.1 Marriage and family therapists are in violation of this Code and subject to termination of membership, or other appropriate action, if they: a) are convicted of a crime substantially related to their professional qualifications or functions; b) are expelled from or disciplined by other professional organizations; c) have their licenses or certificates suspended or revoked or are otherwise disciplined by regulatory bodies; d) if they continue to practice when they are no longer competent to practice because they are impaired due to physical or mental causes or the abuse of alcohol or other substances; or e) fail to cooperate with the Association or the Ethics Committee at any point from the inception of an ethical complaint through the completion of all proceedings regarding that complaint.

3.2 Marriage and family therapists avoid contractual arrangements which provide financial incentives to withhold or limit medically/psychologically necessary care.

3.3 Marriage and family therapists maintain patient records, whether written, taped, computerized, or stored in any other medium, consistent with sound clinical practice.

3.4 Marriage and family therapists seek appropriate professional assistance for their personal problems or conflicts that impair work performance or clinical judgment.

3.5 Marriage and family therapists as teachers, supervisors, and researchers, maintain high standards of scholarship and present accurate information.

3.6 Marriage and family therapists actively strive to understand the diverse cultural backgrounds of their clients by gaining knowledge, personal awareness, and developing sensitivity and skills pertinent to working with a diverse client population.

3.7 Marriage and family therapists are aware of how their cultural/racial/ethnic identity, values and beliefs affect the process of therapy.

3.8 Marriage and family therapists remain abreast of developments in their field through educational activities and clinical experiences.

3.9 Marriage and family therapists do not engage in sexual or other harassment or exploitation of patients, students, interns, trainees, supervisees, employees or colleagues.

3.10 Marriage and family therapists do not assess, test, diagnose, treat, or advise on problems beyond the level of their competence as determined by their education, training and experience. While developing new areas of practice, marriage and family therapists take steps to ensure the competence of their work through education, training, consultation, and/or supervision.

3.11 Marriage and family therapists do not generally provide professional services to a person receiving treatment or therapy from another psychotherapist, except by agreement with such other psychotherapist or after the termination of the patient's relationship with the other psychotherapist.

3.12 Marriage and family therapists take reasonable steps to prevent the distortion or misuse of their clinical and research findings.

3.13 Marriage and family therapists, because of their ability to influence and alter the lives of others, exercise special care when making public their professional recommendations and opinions through testimony or other public statements.

4. RESPONSIBILITY TO STUDENTS AND SUPERVISEES

Marriage and family therapists do not exploit the trust and dependency of students and supervisees.

4.1 Marriage and family therapists are aware of their influential position with respect to students and supervisees, and they avoid exploiting the trust and dependency of such persons. Marriage and family therapists therefore avoid dual relationships that are reasonably likely to impair professional judgment or lead to exploitation. Provision of therapy to students or supervisees is unethical. Provision of marriage and family therapy supervision to clients is unethical. Sexual intercourse, sexual contact or sexual intimacy and/or harassment of any kind with students or supervisees is unethical.

4.2 Marriage and family therapists do not permit students, employees or supervisees to perform or to hold themselves out as competent to perform professional services beyond their training, level of experience, and competence.

4.3 Marriage and family therapists who act as supervisors are responsible for maintaining the quality of their supervision skills, and obtaining consultation or supervision for their work as supervisors whenever appropriate.

5 RESPONSIBILITY TO COLLEAGUES

Marriage and family therapists treat colleagues with respect, courtesy, fairness, and good faith, and cooperate with colleagues in order to promote the welfare and best interests of the patient.

5.1 Marriage and family therapists respect the confidences of colleagues that are shared in the course of their professional relationships.

5.2 Marriage and family therapists are encouraged to assist colleagues who are impaired due to substance abuse, emotional problems, or mental illness.

5.3 Marriage and family therapists do not file or encourage the filing of ethics or other complaints that they know, or reasonably should know, are frivolous.

6. RESPONSIBILITY TO RESEARCH PARTICIPANTS

Investigators respect the dignity and protect the welfare of participants in research and are aware of federal and state laws and regulations and professional standards governing the conduct of research.

6.1 Investigators are responsible for making careful examinations of ethical acceptability in planning studies. To the extent that services to research participants may be compromised by participation in research, investigators seek the ethical advice of qualified professionals not directly involved in the investigation and observe safeguards to protect the rights of research participants.

6.2 Investigators requesting participants' involvement in research inform them of all aspects of the research that might reasonably be expected to influence willingness to participate. Investigators are especially sensitive to the possibility of diminished consent when participants are also receiving clinical services, have impairments which limit understanding and/or communication, or when participants are children.

6.3 Investigators respect participants' freedom to decline participation in or to withdraw from a research study at any time. This obligation requires special thought and consideration when investigators or other members of the research team are in positions of authority or influence over participants. Marriage and family therapists, therefore, make every effort to avoid dual relationships with research participants that could impair professional judgment or increase the risk of exploitation.

6.4 Information obtained about a research participant during the course of an investigation is confidential unless there is an authorization previously obtained in writing. When the possibility exists that others, including family members, may obtain access to such information, this possibility, together with the plan for protecting confidentiality, is explained as part of the procedure for obtaining informed consent.

7. RESPONSIBILITY TO PROFESSION

Marriage and family therapists respect the rights and responsibilities of professional colleagues and participate in activities which advance the goals of the profession.

7.1 Marriage and family therapists remain accountable to the standards of the profession when acting as members or employees of organizations.

7.2 Marriage and family therapists assign publication credit to those who have contributed to a publication in proportion to their contributions and in accordance with customary professional publication practices.

7.3 Marriage and family therapists who are the authors of books or other materials that are published or distributed appropriately cite persons to whom credit for original ideas is due.

7.4 Marriage and family therapists who are the authors of books or other materials published or distributed by an organization take reasonable steps to ensure that the organization promotes and advertises the materials accurately and factually.

7.5 Marriage and family therapists recognize a responsibility to participate in activities that contribute to a better community and society, including devoting a portion of their professional activity to services for which there is little or no financial return.

7.6 Marriage and family therapists are concerned with developing laws and regulations pertaining to marriage and family therapy that serve the public interest, and with altering such laws and regulations that are not in the public interest.

7.7 Marriage and family therapists cooperate with the Ethics Committee and truthfully represent facts to the Ethics Committee. Failure to cooperate with the Ethics Committee is itself a violation of these standards.

8. RESPONSIBILITY TO LEGAL SYSTEM

Marriage and family therapists recognize their role in the legal system and their duty to remain objective and truthful.

8.1 Marriage and family therapists who give testimony in legal proceedings testify truthfully and avoid making misleading statements.

8.2 Marriage and family therapists who act as expert witnesses base their opinions and conclusions on appropriate data, and are careful to acknowledge the limits of their data or conclusions in order to avoid providing misleading testimony or reports.

8.3 Marriage and family therapists avoid, wherever possible, performing conflicting roles in legal proceedings and disclose any potential conflicts to prospective clients, to the courts, or to others as appropriate.

8.4 Marriage and family therapists, regardless of their role in a legal proceeding, remain objective and do not compromise their professional judgment or integrity.

8.5 Marriage and family therapists do not express professional opinions about an individual's mental or emotional condition unless they have conducted an examination of the individual, or unless they reveal the limits of the information upon which their professional opinions are based, with appropriate cautions as to the effects of such limited information upon their opinions.

9. FINANCIAL ARRANGEMENTS

Marriage and family therapists make financial arrangements with patients and supervisees that are understandable and conform to accepted professional practices.

9.1 Marriage and family therapists do not offer or accept payment for referrals.

9.2 Marriage and family therapists do not financially exploit their patients.

9.3 Marriage and family therapists disclose their fees, including charges for canceled or missed appointments and any interest to be charged on unpaid balances, at the beginning of treatment and give reasonable notice of any changes in fees or other charges.

9.4 Marriage and family therapists give reasonable notice to patients with unpaid balances of their intent to sue, or to refer for collection. Whenever legal action is taken, therapists will avoid disclosure of clinical information. Whenever unpaid balances are referred to collection agencies, therapists will exercise care in selecting collection agencies and will avoid disclosure of clinical information.

9.5 Marriage and family therapists ordinarily refrain from accepting goods, services, or other non-monetary remuneration from patients in return for professional services. Such arrangements often create conflicts and may lead to exploitation or distortion of the professional relationship.

9.6 Marriage and family therapists represent facts regarding services rendered fully and truthfully to third party payers.

10. ADVERTISING

Marriage and family therapists engage in appropriate informational activities, including those that enable lay persons to choose professional services on an informed basis.

10.1 Marriage and family therapists accurately represent their competence, education, training, and experience relevant to their professional practice.

10.2 Marriage and family therapists assure that advertisements and publications, whether in directories, announcement cards, newspapers, or on radio or television, are formulated to accurately convey information that is necessary for the public to make an appropriate selection.

10.3 Marriage and family therapists do not use a name which could mislead the public concerning the identity, responsibility, source, and status of those practicing under that name and do not hold themselves out as being partners or associates of a firm if they are not.

10.4 Marriage and family therapists do not use any professional identification (such as a business card, office sign, letterhead, or telephone or association directory listing) if it includes a statement or claim that is false, fraudulent, misleading, or deceptive. A statement is false, fraudulent, misleading, or deceptive if it a) contains a material misrepresentation of fact; b) fails to state any material fact necessary to make the statement, in light of all circumstances, not misleading; or c) is intended to or is likely to create an unjustified expectation.

10.5 Marriage and family therapists correct, wherever possible, false, misleading, or inaccurate information and representations made by others concerning the therapist's qualifications, services, or products.

10.6 Marriage and family therapists do not solicit testimonials from patients.

10.7 Marriage and family therapists make certain that the qualifications of persons in their employ are represented in a manner that is not false, misleading, or deceptive.

10.8 Marriage and family therapists may represent themselves as specializing within a limited area of marriage and family therapy, but only if they have the education, training, and experience which meet recognized professional standards to practice in that specialty area.

10.9 CAMFT clinical, associate and prelicensed members may identify such membership in CAMFT in public information or advertising materials, but they must clearly and accurately represent whether they are clinical, associate, or prelicensed members.

10.10 Marriage and family therapists may not use the initials CAMFT following their name in the manner of an academic degree.

10.11 Marriage and family therapists may use the CAMFT logo only after receiving permission in writing from the Association. Permission will be granted by the Association to CAMFT members in good standing in accordance with Association policy on use of CAMFT logo. The Association (which is the sole owner of its name, logo, and the abbreviated initials CAMFT) may grant permission to CAMFT committees and chartered chapters in good standing, operating as such, to use the CAMFT logo. Such permission will be granted in accordance with Association policy on use of the CAMFT logo.

10.12 Marriage and family therapists use their membership in CAMFT only in connection with their clinical and professional activities.

Violations of these standards should be brought to the attention of the CAMFT Ethics Committee, in writing, at CAMFT's administrative office, 7901 Raytheon Road, San Diego, CA 92111-1606, or at such other address as may be necessary because of a change in location of the administrative office.

[i] The terms psychotherapy, therapy and counseling are used interchangeably throughout the Ethical Standards.

[ii] The word "patient," as used herein, is synonymous with such

words as "client" or "counselee."

[iii] The term "marriage and family therapist," as used herein, is synonymous with the term "licensed marriage, family and child counselor," and is intended to cover registered interns and trainees doing marriage, family and child counseling under supervision.

[iv] Dual relationships include multiple relationships with patients.

Approved by CAMFT Board of Directors 4/4/97
Effective date 6/7/97

Index

N

O

P

R

S

T

V

W

Dr. Barbara Lipinski is a licensed psychologist and licensed marriage, family, and child therapist. She is a member of the core faculty at Pacifica Graduate Institute and serves as the Clinical Coordinator of the Counseling Psychology Program. She received her doctorate at the University of Southern California and is a clinical member of the American Psychological Association, the California Association of Marriage and Family Therapists, The American Professional Society on the Abuse of Children, the California Psychological Association, and the American Academy of Police Psychology. She is a Diplomate of the American Board of Forensic Examiners, Life Fellow of the American College of Forensic Examiners, and served on the Executive Advisory Board of the American Psychotherapy Association. Part of her recent sabbatical included a voyage to Australia.